BORN TO HEAL ME

HOW TO MOVE FORWARD WHEN YOU FEEL LIKE YOU'RE OUT OF OPTIONS

Prominence Publishing
www.prominencepublishing.com

Born to Heal Me / Michael-Don Smith -- 1st ed.

ISBN: 978-1-990830-18-1

What People Are Saying

I had the privilege to read a pre-publication copy of 'BORN TO HEAL ME', and I have to say, it was an incredibly powerful and transformative experience. The 8 stories in this book are not only incredibly inspiring, but they also hit home in a very relatable way. The vulnerability and honesty of the individuals featured in the stories is incredibly moving and their experiences will leave you feeling a deep emotional and spiritual connection. Each story left me feeling uplifted and renewed, and by the end of the book, I felt empowered to take control of my own healing journey. The title of the book itself is fitting, as it is incomplete and as you read, you will understand the true meaning of the message, and it will resonate with you. I highly recommend this book to anyone who is seeking inspiration, motivation, and healing in their life. It is a true self-development gm.

Air Commodore Dr Marcia McLaughlin F.Birm.Soc,
Editor In Chief / CEO at The Phoenix Newspaper

This compelling, easy-to-read book is about taking care of your health. It is honest and real. It is a must-read for anyone facing long-term health challenges and everyone who wants to live a long, happy, healthy life. It tells true stories of people who have faced demanding situations and shows how they overcame them. It covers the reality of illnesses, how to recover, how to prevent them, and how to persevere. The book offers practical advice and tools for healing and growth, and helps readers navigate the fast-paced and often unkind culture of ableism. It will empower and guide readers on their journey to overcome obstacles and achieve success and robust vitality in their lives."

Dr Mark Esho MBE, DBA, Multi Award-Winning Entrepreneur, Director at Easy Internet Services, Easy Internet Solutions, Dreme, Access Rating CIC

TABLE OF CONTENTS

Born to Heal Me

By Michael-Don Smith

"We are all ready to win, just as we are born knowing only life. It is defeat that you must learn to prepare for."

- Bruce Lee, Enter the Dragon

You were born with the innate, magical, unlimited ability to heal yourself after trauma. Because a full life is made up of trauma and stress and dangerous 'stuff,' you had to be made that way. Take a moment and consider all the everyday miracles the human machine performs routinely with no instruction or assistance from the owner. It would seem obvious and almost redundant to remind any sensible individual, 'take good care of your body, and it will grow, work, and heal itself for a long, healthy life.' We are each born with an effortless thirst for life; it is our hunger for health we must strive to develop.

Born after A Stroke!

"The soul always knows what to do to heal itself. The challenge is to silence the mind."

– Caroline Myss

Before the age of 2, he couldn't see, hear, smell, taste, or feel. His name, well, let's call him Mr. X. We met at an open mic event where I was reading some of my poetry, and he was playing guitar. He was 19 years old when we met, and even at that young age, he was already a brilliant musician. His love was Classical Blues, and apparently, according to better-qualified members of the audience, 'his chops were on-point.' In more everyday words, he played with consummate and effortless skill. The kind of talent rarely seen outside of Ronnie Scots on a professional stage or perhaps a YouTube video with a million-plus views. I approached him and asked him if he would accompany me as I read one of my poems, a normal request at these 'gigs' where artists love the creativity of 'jamming.' He kindly agreed, and a wonderful friendship was born.

One day I asked 'out of the blue' if he had a perfect pitch. It is not unusual for musical prodigies to be able to hear a note and know precisely which note it is, and hearing a piece of music, know the exact musical key. No, he didn't have perfect pitch, but he did have the ability to see a different colour for each note. This is a rare condition/ability called synaesthesia, where one sense, such as taste or smell, when stimulated, simultaneously triggers the perception of another unstimulated sense (e.g., colour). Mr. X went on, "before I was born, I had a stroke in my mother's womb. And I was affected by severe ill health early on in life, and now I am really, really grateful for all my senses." In fact, for him, practising for weeks and months to be able to say one word means that working on his music for three hours a day for days on end is no big deal. Because he really appreciates his gifts and the miracle that somehow his brain and body had repaired itself. From a devastating situation for the mother and family, which they were told was incurable and her son would never have a normal life.

According to Dr. Joe Dispenza, spontaneous remission, brain plasticity, and the placebo effect, all have one thing in common, they describe the transition from an ineffective state to an effective state by the unassisted, unaccountable, unconscious, and autonomous restructuring and repair of the bodies psychology, physiology, and neurology.

Spontaneous remission means one had some incurable disease or health disorder, and it went away without or even despite conventional medical treatment. In Native American Traditional Healing Systems, they say this happens when something shifts within our own consciousness to connect/re-connect us with nature to create profound self-actualised healing.

A Stroke from Nowhere?

"If by gaining knowledge we destroy our health,
we labour for a thing that will be useless in our hands."

– John Locke

It was the morning of the 13th of July 2016, the 195th day of the year in the Gregorian calendar. There were 171 days remaining until the end of the year. The day of the week was Wednesday, and I mysteriously struggled to raise the spoon of crunchy nut cornflakes to my mouth. I had no idea that this would be the last time I would ever use my right hand to feed myself for a long time.

Look up the definition of stress; you may be surprised at how many definitions there are for this word. This is an indication of how important and prevalent stress is in our lives. The word comes from the shortening of 'distress,' from Old French 'estresse' translated as narrowness and/or oppression, based on Latin strictus 'drawn tight.' So one way it can be defined is by the denoting pressure or force exerted on a person for the purpose of initiating unwilling change. This definition is useful as it includes the remedy for stress, which is change. In fact, if you don't make the appropriate change, the stress will become more intense until the change makes itself.

I remember thinking as I was pouring the ice-cold cow's milk into my bowl of super-sweet cornflakes. You are a hero, Mr. Smith. It's only Wednesday, and you've already driven to important meetings in Leeds from Birmingham twice, made the Birmingham to Plymouth return journey yesterday with a quick emergency client meeting in Leicester, and now, having averaged 4 to 5 hours of sleep a day for… well face it that's the norm most days, you are still chasing new clients and closing big deals like a 35-year-old. You're good!

If only I'd known "One of the symptoms of an approaching nervous breakdown is the belief that one's work is terribly important."

– Bertrand Russell

Yes, that was the morning my silent unattended stress decided not to wait for me to change any longer and to introduce me to a whole new world of pain by way of a Middle Cerebral Artery (MCA) stroke. The MCA is by far the largest cerebral artery and is the vessel most commonly affected by a cerebrovascular accident. Who knew? It happened suddenly, without warning. To my pre-stroke self, that shocking incident absolutely came out of nowhere.

We tend to think of strokes happening to older people. But every year, in developed countries, about 10 to 15 percent of strokes occur in children and adults under age 45, and that number is rising.

There are two types of stroke: ischemic and haemorrhagic. The biggest increase is seen in ischemic strokes resulting from artery-blocking blood clots that travel to the brain.

Are you at risk of having a stroke? The fact is, anyone can have a stroke, from infants to seniors. If you're under 60, the likelihood is small. After age 60, the risk starts to increase. Why? Because it's what you do and don't do habitually over time that puts your name on the waiting list for a stroke.

But there's one stroke statistic that's downright shocking: More than 90% of strokes are preventable.

"If you ask me what is the single most important key to longevity, I would have to say it is avoiding worry, stress, and tension. And if you didn't ask me, I'd still have to say it."

— George Burns

A Flash of Genius

On the 13th of July 2016, I had a stroke. Physically it took away half my body, which was quite annoying, but the bad bit was I lost the ability to speak. For somebody who makes [made?] a living as a public speaker, that's a bit inconvenient. The good news was that I was back on stage speaking within eight weeks of my Transient Ischaemic Attack (TIA). My youngest son had to pour me onto the platform, my right arm was in a sling, and I didn't move far from where he left me during the talk, but I was back!

What I'd really like to share with you is my 55 years in the making, Flash Of Genius.* At the time of writing, it's been over five years since my brain injury. Although I was speaking again within 2 or 3 months, it was 3 years before I was walking freely. I am still at 70 to 80% recovery with my Cornflakes hand, but confident I will get to 100% plus of my pre-stroke functionality.

I am convinced that the reason I was able to recover my speech so quickly, compared to my other abilities, is that I had spent over 30 years speaking and presenting and speaking and presenting. Through that deliberate practice over an extended period of time, I built up an extraordinary level of connected neurology; nerve cells, axons, dendrites, myelin sheathing, etc., all the thinking and performing 'chops' associated with public speaking. So much rhetoric referencing mental real estate that the stroke couldn't take it all away. It also meant I was able to 'Build Back Better' the destroyed areas quite quickly. I thought, why did I do that so quickly while others struggle for years or never recover their speech. My amateur conclusion was that because speaking was how I made my living, I was much more intentional and focused in this area than the majority.

Unknowingly I had earned the benefits of Deep Practice. One of my childhood heroes was Bruce Lee, and he said, "I do not fear the warrior who was practiced a thousand kicks, I fear the one who has practiced one kick a thousand times." That's the power of deliberate Deep Practice over time. You build incredible resilience on numerous levels. There are things you do often and regularly that have incredible value in your life. Those are where your greatest resilience lies. By now, you should at least be considering adding significant health and well-being practices to your list of non-negotiable must-do items on your daily schedule.

*The acronym for **Flash of Genius** is **FOG** 😊

A Stroke of Insight

"The real secret to lifelong good health is actually counterintuitive: Don't command, listen. Let your body take care of you."

– Deepak Chopra

Healthy mind Healthy body, Heal-thy mind Heal-thy Body

"Your body holds deep wisdom. Trust in it. Learn from it. Nourish it. Watch your life transform and be healthy."

– Bella Bleue

The more invested we become in technology and external forces to support our health and healing, the further we move away from our natural capability. The next time you have a minor scrape or scratch, notice how the body is able to marshall the required resources to heal the wound. Below skin level, it is constantly engaged in a war. A war on your behalf where you seem, in general, reluctant to help and instead play the role of spectator.

Hippocrates said, "healing is a matter of time and of opportunity." Time refers to patience listening to your body, and not trying to rush things. Opportunity refers to ensuring that your body has everything it needs to heal. Here Hippocrates says, "let your food be your medicine and your medicine be your food." Your body will heal itself with your help in providing the best resources through your diet. I would encourage you to eat natural FROGS regularly. If you ensure your diet is 80% Fresh, Ripe, Organic, Green, and Simple, the odds are you will have everything it needs. And that really is the greatest insight I gained from my experience with stroke. You can heal you. It may take a week, a month, or 10 years. But given time, your body will heal. I hope you find these words useful. And they help you to live a wonderful, happy, and joyful life.

Express Love, Gratitude, and Kindness And Stay Blessed

Please take very, very special care of you. Your gifts are many and unique, your potential is limitless, there is only one of you, and the infinite, eternal universe will never ever get the chance to do you again.

Love Comes Down

Autumn leaves limbless fall down.
Once green with life connected sure
Certain that certain things don't change.
And reality is life and growth and love,
A little boy skips and kicks dead leaves with joy
And laughs as mommy prays he won't trip up.

She recalls he gave her up
Lover's promises of forever let her down
And left her low with growing joy,
That strong would leave her weak for sure.
Like the fair that from itself declines is love,
Blind destiny just another word like change.

Who, like sudden spring, can change?
The heart's frozen winter and warm up
Ice cold indifference and rekindle love?
Rather hate than this nothing that holds her down.
Security a cracked mirror that cannot be sure
It's illusion of safety will ever return joy

Summers strength, heat, and embrace, that joy
Power and redoubtable resolve defying change,
Can anyone, any dream again be that sure?
A young woman with sleepy eyes smiles as she wakes up.
She shivers and says she thinks the down
Feels chilly, and snuggles closer to her true love.
It was meant to be, she whispers to love

Know that you are my eternal joy,
There is no better, though heaven come down.
A little boy asleep, dreams of winning for a change
Of a time, a place, a person who stands to help him up
Who says and means and lives 'of me you can be sure.'

On the shifting deck, seasoned feet are sure,
A man is either quick or dead in love
Life holds on to all the choices we will not give up.
From the joy, we build for others comes our joy
The laws of nature flatter and dissemble, and never change
Woman or Man, the one you hold up cannot let you down.

Never give up, on the seeds of joy,
They are sure as life and their fruit is love
And their only change is to draw more love down. -TSToCD

About the Author

Michael-Don Smith CPS, CMC, MPNLP

As a Business Mentor, Social Entrepreneur, Educator and Speaker, Michael-Don 'Don' commands a remarkable breadth of knowledge and experience in business & life.

His career has seen him travel all over the world, engaging with many cultures professionally and personally, including significant contributions in military, corporate and charitable Sectors.

In the Royal Air Force, he studied and taught Electronics and Avionics, followed as a Telecom Engineer and Corporate Project Manager at Cable & Wireless Worldwide PLC.

His first company [X-Tek Ltd], an independent management consultancy, was started during the 'dot com' boom in the late 1990s. This organisation was developed and transformed into his current award winning personal and business development company Mindstyle.

Don works with individuals and organisations, focusing on; creating a powerful and effective Business Value Proposition, human communication skills and modern leadership. He delivers in a way that is tailored and specific to each client and consistently delivers fast, measurable and outstanding results.

His secret passion is writing poetry, '... *since the age of 10 I've been writing poetry and after 50 years I bowed to the requests of the trusted few who have read some of my work and published a small selection of what I hope will provide entertainment while provoking questions and second thoughts on the part of those who take the time to read 'The secret thoughts of chairman Don'.*

Publications available on Amazon:

- *Success Secrets for Wellbeing: with Penny Power OBE and 10 World-Class Expert Authors*
- *Rugby Insight: Mental Health to Mental Wealth: with Mr A N Smith MSc*
- *The Secret Thoughts of Chairman Don: An Eclectic Selection of Original Poetry and Prose*
- *Easy as NLP*
- *Success Mindstyle*
- *Reach 4 Balance*

Connect with Michael-Don:

don@craftyoursignaturespeech.com

www.CraftYourSignatureSpeech.com

LinkedIn.com/in/MichaelDonSmith

Barbara in Wonderland

By Barbara Emanuel

I was born and bred in the heart of the West Midlands, with a rich mix of cultures and proverbs. One proverb that stands out for me is "God don't come, but he sends," an old Black country saying which means when you are down on your luck, you are not forgotten and that even though God cannot come in person, someone or something will arrive to guide and support you. There is also a Caribbean saying that is very similar, which is "God nah sleep." This means that all wrongs done to you will be righted, a form of Karma, again stressing that you are being watched over, that justice will prevail, and that you will rise again.

The theme here is that God is always ahead of our needs, desires, and hardships. I say God, but you may have your own belief systems, which can be replaced here. The Caribbean culture I belong to has at its heart a belief that the universe has pre-ordained plans for us and, as such, will place you in the right location, at the right time, to achieve your destiny. For me, God has always sent books; it has always been the right book at the right time, along with some amazing people to facilitate my journey and personal growth. I have used these books again and again to assist me in deciphering difficult situations in my life or in contributing to my spiritual growth.

There were times in my life when disappointments led me to experience low self-worth, which in turn generated thoughts of a negative nature. The first time was while undergoing fertility treatments which spanned 7 years. Often the procedures were invasive, and the results disappointing. I was married at the time to a man who was single-minded and pragmatic, while I, on the other hand, was giving and supportive. However, when I needed him most, he lacked the empathy and compassion I needed to endure my plight. Instead, he spent the entire period reminding me of my inability to conceive naturally.

I had already given birth to our wonderful, bright, and intelligent son and desperately wanted to complete my family with another child. However, as a maternal-focused woman, I felt a great sense of loss and disappointment in my body; it had let me down badly. For me, the process of getting pregnant appeared biologically simple, and yet, it was not happening for me. My final options were to undergo courses of assisted conception, failing those IVF treatments at a neighbouring hospital.

The whole process of undergoing fertility treatment is a complete act of faith. There are no guarantees of success. In fact, women are told from the start that there is only a 60% chance of success. I prayed I would be one of the 60%. What inspired me most while undergoing the process was the non-judgemental way we were treated by the medical team and the fact that every woman there was in the same boat. Plus, the amazing collage of babies conceived from women undergoing various fertility treatments. The numerous photos were placed in a predominant position on the waiting room wall, for all to see. As I looked up at them, I promised myself that one day a photograph of my baby would be placed on that wall, as a celebration of my faith and tenacity.

Even so, there were times when out shopping, I would see pregnant women everywhere, some even having two and three young children in tow. In those moments, my world would fall apart, as I longed to conceive, bear a child, and prove my womanhood, once and for all. Most of all, the longing was for my then-husband to take me into his arms and, with kind words, reassure me that everything would be ok. Instead, I had to endure a daily torrent of put-downs and ridicule from someone that was supposed to love me.

Despite working full-time in a responsible job and coming from a supportive and loving family, there was an overwhelming feeling of despair and worthlessness. Slowly, negative thoughts crept into my psyche. They were irrational, based on self-pity, and often sudden and uninvited. I tried to balance the perceived worthlessness of the woman at home with the strong, capable woman the world knew me to be.

So, now, I am sharing my experiences for all women experiencing infertility and those in relationships that steal their self-worth.

At my lowest point, God sent me one particular book, and over the years, several other books found their way to me mysteriously. A list of some of the books will be provided at the end of this chapter. The first book was "Feel the Fear and Do it Anyway" by Susan Jeffers (1987). This book came to me when I most needed it to heal my self-doubt and build my self-esteem. The core of the book explores how to turn fears and indecision into action.

On this particular journey, I say this, as I have had other life-changing experiences that enabled me to learn the spiritual lessons required to make me the rounded and highly capable person I am today. Therefore, I want to reassure you that life is a continuous process of disappointments, exploration, and learning. You may find that as we get over one hurdle or turn a bend, something else comes along to test your resolve. For me, the books that found their way to me provided ongoing reference materials, tools, and insights to enable me to heal myself.

Here I was, alone physically and emotionally, lost in a sea of unanswered questions. Being totally alone to cope with my infertility, I had to develop my inner strength and the skills to carry me through without the option of turning to self-harm or depression. I needed help to develop a host of qualities. I required resilience, enhanced self-esteem, and inner confidence. The universe saw my plight and gifted this incredible book to me, which laid out a series of tools and models which could be applied to my circumstances perfectly.

Now I had the strategies to handle situations that previously caused pain, paralysis, and depression. This was achieved by tapping into my internal resources to create excitement, energy, and power, as alternative emotions. The three main tools I used and want to share with you are as follows:

Tool 1 – The Chatterbox

I was amazed to find I had a Chatterbox in my head, implying that I was weak and often repeating what my then-husband was saying to me – "you're barren," "you're the one with the problem, not me." Basically, "I am ok. You are not ok." This negativism, combined with my own negative self-beliefs, allowed my Chatterbox to generate fear and paralysis, which in turn prevented me from generating hope for the future. In fact, the Chatterbox was keeping me a prisoner of my own insecurities.

Try these practical tips!

Task 1

- Start by identifying your Chatterbox. Then, note down what your Chatterbox is saying to you? I can bet it is not saying, "go for it!" or "you're wonderful!" Instead, you may find it tends to be a reminder of past failures and embarrassments.

- Decide the extent to which each statement listed is holding you back from being the wonderful human being you were born to be.

- Once you have recognised and are fully aware of the Chatterbox, you will be ready for Tool 2. Mapping how much pain you are in, in any given situation and changing your internal vocabulary into one that reduces fear and allows you to take action.

Tool 2 - Pain to Power

The Pain to Power tool allows the acknowledgement of held insecurities by giving you the opportunity to plot your level of pain or power in any given situation. This can be based on your internal dialogue or held emotions surrounding the situation.

My healing came from understanding and managing my internal dialogue. I had to learn to speak to myself with kindness and love. The alternative was to let the Chatterbox play on and on like a broken record. I achieved this by retraining my inner dialogue, which changed how I viewed myself. Knowing how to use this tool to empower ourselves is how we can best curb the Chatterbox. The aim is to eliminate the pain and, by so doing so, eradicate inertia.

Examples of how to transition from Pain to Power:

Pain	------------------------▶	Power
I cannot		I will not
I should		I could
What will I do?		I know I can handle this
Life's a struggle		Life's an adventure
If only		Next time

The examples in the left-hand column suggest that we have no control over our lives. The right-hand column puts the individual in the realm of personal choice. The Chatterbox and our internal vocabulary are often ruled by our subconscious mind, which believes what is registered within it. Having personal affirmations such as "I am strong," "I am powerful," and "I am loved" are important in reinforcing our self-worth. Strong affirmations prevent our subconscious mind from making choices based on weakness, which can affect our ability to deal with whatever life has to throw at us.

This tool was life-changing for me, as I was unaware that I had a Chatterbox and, even more so, of its negative programming. In addition,I was aware that I was in pain, but had no idea how much pain, or indeed how to stop being a "victim" and create movement in my life. The first thing I had to do was to disarm the Chatterbox and build a strong dialogue based on self-love, self-respect, and self-regard. This allowed me to stop complaining and instead sculpting my life. I started developing and working with spiritual laws, setting goals, and taking action.

Tool 3 - Expanding your Comfort Zone

Using the "Pain to Power Chart" made me realise that one of my greatest fears was following through on the decision to leave my marriage, it was not empowering me. I could no longer live with the feelings of helplessness, the fear of wondering what people would say, or being seen as a social failure. Yes, I was afraid, but by using the Comfort Zone Model within the book, I found it was possible to take small incremental steps, when moving from a position of "pain to power" which allowed me to achieve my goals with ease. I found fear can be managed, risks minimized and next steps less overwhelming.

An illustration of the model can be found below:

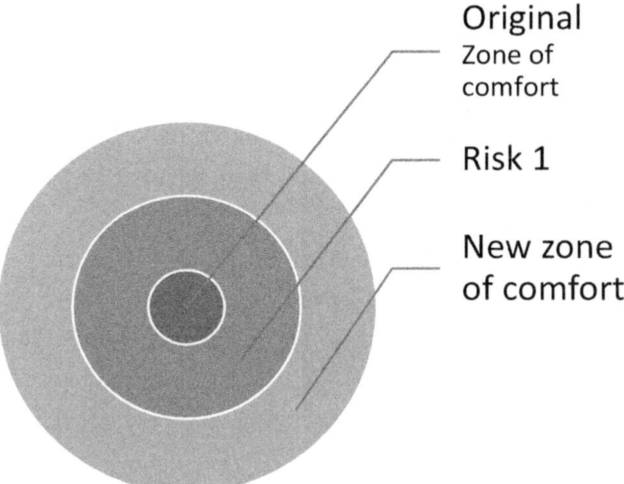

This model is about taking several small risks that aim to enhance self-confidence and personal accomplishments. You will find, as I did, that by taking small safe risks, there is nothing to fear but fear itself. By using the model, I soon became so far removed from my original comfort zone, that I took pleasure in setting further smaller goals which when combined enabled me to achieve my desired outcome.

Task 2

- Make a list of some of your fears and set yourself small challenges. It could be as simple as having a coffee alone or going to a show or attending a course you always wanted to complete.

Reflections

My life today is a million miles away from the struggles of attempting to conceive a child. I am now a qualified and accomplished Learning and Development Practitioner and qualified Coach. I have achieved several academic qualifications by remaining focused and taking small steps within my zone of comfort.

I also gained an MBA, despite being pregnant with my second child. My family is now complete, and I could not be prouder of my two sons. Whom I raised alone as a single, divorced parent. Feeling the fear and doing it anyway helped me heal my broken spirit, take control of my life, and grab opportunities that presented themselves.

The title of this chapter is Barbara in Wonderland; in fact, it could easily have been "Barbara in Horror Land." Alice`s challenges and numerous adventures were horrendous to me. However, the writer requested that we look at her journey through a different lens. One of choice, excitement, and action. I can relate to the story of Alice in Wonderland well. I, too, followed a rabbit down a hole, cried rivers of tears, lost perceptive, and had to stand up for myself. At times, I too, was either too big or too small for the situation I found myself in. But just like Alice, I learned the 'lessons so they would lessen.' Finally, and gloriously just like Alice, I became brave and strong, and I found my voice and moved from a place of pain to power.

By using the tools and models within "Feel the Fear and Do it Anyway" (1987), I found increased confidence to act. I hope this chapter has been relatable and inspiring and that you, too, can use the tools, models, and tasks outlined to assess the challenges in your life. I trust that I have given you the confidence and courage to seek out new opportunities and in turn, be rewarded with an outlook that generates endless possibilities.

Recommended Books

- *The Value in the Valley: A Black Woman's Guide Through Life's Dilemmas* – Iyanla Vanzant
- *One Day my Soul Opened Up: Working Toward Spiritual Strength and Personal Growth* – Iyanla Vanzant
- *In the Meantime: Finding Yourself and the Love You Want* – Iyanla Vanzant
- *Acts of Faith: Meditations for People of Colour* – Iyanla Vanzant
- *The life You Were Born to Live: A Guide to Finding Your Life Purpose* – Dan Millman
- *The Boy, the Mole, the Fox and the Horse* – Charlie Mackesy
- *How to Live When You Could be Dead* – Deborah James
- *You Can Heal Your Life* – Louise Hay
- *The Power is Within You* – Louise Hay
- *Feel the Fear and Do it Anyway: Dynamic Techniques for Turning Fear, Indecision, and Anger into Power, Action, and Love* – Susan Jeffers
- *Alice in Wonderland* – Lewis Carroll

About the Author

Barbara is an experienced and talented Learning and Development specialist. She lectures and facilitates workshops nationally. Covering topics such as Equality and Diversity, Personal Development, Team Building, Oranisational Development and Leadership Development. Her mission is to assist in the empowerment of all people, allowing them to reach their full potential by using a range of accredited self-assessment tools, education, coaching and mentoring.

Barbara believes in the power of education and self-development, she loves learning. She holds a number of academic degrees, an MBA, a Level 8 qualification in leadership and research, as well as an ILM Level 7 qualification in Coaching and Mentoring. Barbara is a skilled practitioner in a number of psychometric testing tools. Barbara is also a trained Mediator.

Barbara has a strong creative ability; she designed, narrated and produced a series of productions which she delivered in support of International Women's week annually. Barbara used her creative talents to reinterrupt the stories of Shirley Valentine, Alice in Wonderland and Over the Rainbow, using poetry, song, dance and storytelling to ensure the narratives of each story remained magical and relatable to the lives of women today.

Connect with Barbara:

barbara@barbara-emanuel.com

www.Barbara-Emanuel.com

LinkedIn.com/in/Barbara-Emanuel-6672a436/

Vocation – Diary of a Failed Trainee Priest

By Des McCabe

I lay motionless, my face pressed against the cold tiled floor in the boys' toilets at my secondary school, pretending to be unconscious. I certainly wasn't going to get up and fight three of my classmates. I hoped they would just go away, and they did.

Teenage years are rarely straightforward, but my search for who I was at sixteen and what I wanted to do, seemed to annoy and indeed disappoint most of those around me.

I was different from the rest of the class because I was thinking of becoming a priest. They were planning to be doctors and dentists, engineers and teachers. I was the 'Holy Joe' of the class.

I had this passion that I could become a missionary, go to Africa, and help those who were hungry and starving. The idea of being a missionary priest seemed to connect me to God and help people in a practical way. It wasn't just a teenage phase.

Much to the dismay and ultimate disappointment of my parents, I spent a couple of weekends at the local retreat centre for the SMA (Society of Missions to Africa) to find out more about their work.

I was slowly 'coming out,' and I knew I had to shift my personality completely if I was to survive at school. From a shy and restrained 16-year-old, I became deliberately outgoing and, indeed, at times, outrageous. Deep down, I was the same person, but I sought to take the world 'head-on' in a determined and upfront way rather than be swamped or intimidated by the response of my schoolmates and others. My quiet ambitions of priesthood, marked by an earlier introverted and reflective nature, became an advance warning system. Des McCabe is the one going to be a priest.

I still enjoyed all of the 'normal' teenage activities, including alcohol and weekend nights out. I had an amazing girlfriend, Sonia. And anyway, it wasn't time for me to head off yet!

My parents couldn't understand it. There were no priests in the family, and although my mother was religious, it was a quiet personal spirituality. They had both worked so hard to get three of us through school. Education, to my mother, was the ultimate gift. In her day, she was the first girl to get the 11+ and have a place at secondary school. There was little chance back then of a university place for working-class Catholic girls in Northern Ireland.

Her ambition for me was to be a doctor. My younger brother Cathal was to be a lawyer. However, he quickly found his true vocation as a gifted writer and poet. With a first-class degree in English and a doctorate from Oxford, I'm so glad I wasn't following in his footsteps! By the time it got to our younger sister Eimear, she was reasonably free to choose her own career! Eimear went to Sheffield University and became a wonderful speech therapist supporting vulnerable people with voice problems.

Anyway, back to 1974. My parents hoped I would grow out of the priest idea. I didn't, and to their credit, when the chips were down, they backed me at every stage. I was so conscious of them trying to explain my decision to their friends.

I remember sitting in the school chapel, just sitting there in silence. Looking back, I think this is where I learned that prayer is silence, words are not needed, and God is within us, not out there somewhere. I have always been looked after. I've always been guided by those liberating words of St Ignatius, who said, 'just do what works for you.'

I still went through the normal University application process where you had to list five choices. I applied for four medicine courses and a fifth choice in psychology. Right up to the point where I would leave school, there was always a chance I would change my mind. This was the insurance policy that I would have somewhere to go. It was also a hope that this was where I would go.

When my A-level results came out, I was in Lincolnshire, England, for the summer as a student, working 12-hour shifts in a canning factory for fruit and vegetables. We all lived in tents. It was the typical teenage freedom in the 1970s.

My Mum expected that I would get three 'A's or something close. She opened the post that August Saturday morning and read the results to me 'live' over the phone. One E (the lowest possible pass) in Maths and two O's (fail) in Physics and Chemistry. It was probably the lowest point in the whole process. I struggled that weekend to cope with the level of personal disappointment and embarrassment (with relatives and friends) that this would cause her. Neither of my parents could understand how I had apparently worked so hard and yet done so abysmally. They were frustrated, annoyed, and bitterly disappointed. I had so let them down.

In my tent in Wisbech, Valerie got the whole story. Lovely Valerie just sat with me and rescued me. She was my angel that day.

I did try to study. I sat in the attic at home for hours every night, but A-level chemistry, physics, and maths were never of any interest to me. My Dad had turned his photography space into a proper study and even paid for a maths tutor (which probably resulted in my one passing grade).

So, off I went to Wilton in Cork in September 1975 for my foundation year with the SMA. I was the most outrageous there, but all the guys were carrying their own struggle with personal identity and their search for vocation in their own way.

The camaraderie and friendship were wonderful. There were twenty-three of us from across Ireland and the UK. We had as much fun as was possible without girls and pubs! As well as daily lessons, we did sports, played games, organised dramas and concerts, and had various outings.

We got up at six every morning for silent prayer and meditation in the chapel from 6:30am to 7:30am. I was never good at the meditation thing, never practised it, and was never taught it. Getting up at that time meant that most mornings, I struggled simply to keep awake. There was little praying.

My first written assignment on 'What is Prayer?' failed Fr Ford's marking system miserably. I thought it was a rare work of theological significance.

I got regular letters from home telling me all the news and missing me. My Mum, Auntie Eileen, and Sonia all wrote regularly. I went home for Christmas but left soon after that. I was the second person to leave. I never discussed it with anyone. I just went in and had a chat with Fr Ford. He asked if the reason was a girlfriend back at home, but it wasn't. To this day, I still cannot say why I left or why I left at that time.

A total of seven of us left in that first year, plus two others who went off to different religious orders. My plan was to go back home, sign on for unemployment benefits on Tuesday, and then take it from there. Unfortunately, my parents had other ideas.

I went back to the same school and became a Boarder. The idea was that maybe the school could help me to learn better if I was closely supervised. I was locked up from Monday to Friday and got to go home on the weekends. Those in the A-level class were now all a year younger than me, of course, so I was by far the oldest in the school. My 'status' of failed priesthood being lived out in a school run by priests was weird for me, although they were kind. It was the sense of isolation in the school and the continued lack of interest in the subjects that made it a tough few months. I didn't enjoy it.

Given that there were less than five months of the academic year remaining, the plan was for me to re-sit Physics and Maths in the hope that I would get into any course at University. Chemistry was seen as a total lost cause.

My re-sit grades did improve. I shifted my Physics from a fail to a basic pass (E), and my Maths rocketed from an E to a D. I scraped onto a course at Ulster University called 'Computer Science' through a process of Clearing – essentially being placed in available courses that others didn't want.

The University intake team knew that I really wanted to do Psychology, and the week before I was due to start, they generously offered me a place on a new four-year honours degree course. At long last, I was doing what

I really enjoyed with amazing new friends. During the placement year, I was fortunate to spend four months at Great Ormond Street Hospital working with very young children with behavioural problems and later worked at an assessment centre in Belfast for 'troubled youths.'

I graduated on schedule with a 2:1 honours degree, and my parents got a very well-earned graduation day.

I wanted to go on and do a Masters in Personnel Management at the University of Aston Business School in Birmingham. My Mum was keen to re-mortgage our little terraced house to pay the fees, but my Dad persuaded his sister Molly (who owned a pub and had no children of her own) to contribute 50%. I then received a 50% scholarship from the University itself.

My Mum wrote to me every week or so, with all the news from home about Cathal and Eimear, about her job and what was happening with the neighbours, the relatives, and my former schoolmates. She was an amazing writer, and I always felt that she was beside me, telling me all the news and gossip! Each letter also contained cash from her job as a librarian. I have kept all her letters.

Immediately after finishing my course, in January 1982, I got my first job with Asda Superstores as a trainee personnel manager. It took me three buses every morning to get to Bloxwich, which was one of the most deprived areas in the West Midlands. I got on well with all the staff, who were mainly young girls on the shop floor. However, my friendly, chatty approach didn't match the 'do not talk to the staff unless you have to' managerial style of my boss in her M&S tweed skirt. She sacked me after six months.

I went back to Northern Ireland and found out that my Mum was dying of ovarian cancer. She had struggled with her illness for almost two years but held out from telling many people for as long as she could, except for my Dad and a few relatives who helped her through her treatment. She never made it to my second graduation day.

I came back to the Midlands and set up my first training business for the unemployed, which didn't get off to a good start. Trevor, my business partner and Financial Director, ran off with all of the £70,000 that we had received as an advance grant. I was on honeymoon in Tenerife at the time. It wasn't the best way to kick off married life; putting it mildly, the Government officials weren't too impressed either. My wife Pauline made me promise to go and get a proper job for six months before thinking about starting a business again. She's been a pretty good influence on me over the years.

And so, I got a job as a Sales Training Manager with Scrivens to teach people how to sell hearing aids. I'd never been in selling before, but a few books on sales techniques helped me to put a good course together. I did ok with Scrivens.

So, where does the diary bit fit in?

I guess I got my interest in writing from my Mum. It certainly wasn't from school. My first efforts were a collection of teenage song lyrics that I wrote when I was 19. The writing process got me into the habit of harvesting and capturing thoughts, ideas, and reflections. I have continued to write over the years, and my first book, "*Work it Out! How to Find the Work You Always Wanted in a Shifting Jobs Market,*" was published by Hay House in 2011. I dedicated it 'To Ma and Da, with love.'

The arrival of Covid on the 24th of March 2020 was a watershed moment for many of us. We didn't know whether it would last a week, a month, or even longer. It was against this background of uncertainty and talk of a "new normal" that I decided to write something every morning from that day onwards.

I chose to get up at 6 o'clock every morning and sit in silence before the chaos of the day arrived. I had no plan, just to write whatever came. Pauline thought I was mad, but the arrival of a morning cup of tea (at a more civilised time) seemed to buy me some leeway.

These pieces became my first-ever diary. Who starts a diary when they are 63? Anyway, the idea was to encourage others to think differently about everything. I took everyday words or phrases and gave a different perspective on each of these. I posed a question or two at the end of each piece to encourage participation in the process. Wearing my trainer's hat, I saw these more as interactive exercises rather than passive reflections.

I took my inspiration from Saint Ignatius of Loyola, who created Spiritual Exercises based on the life of Christ. Ignatius gets us involved as participants in the story rather than just onlookers.

My diary, "Thinking differently about Everything," was born as a daily blog and was posted every day on Facebook, Instagram, and LinkedIn. The first three books of 200 'Inverted Pyramid Exercises' have now been published.

It's difficult to choose a personal favourite, but I have included one at the end of this chapter called 'Vocational Guidance,' which seemed appropriate. It's much longer than all the others, but it captures a lot of what I have learned over the years.

When I was young, I used to think of vocation in career terms. In my case, it might have been a doctor, lawyer, or priest. But now I think that vocation is a direction of travel that shows every day who we are and where we are. Some tough learning early on in my life enabled me to be more self-sufficient, more determined to do the work that matters to me, more willing to take a risk, and happy not always to follow the expectations of others. For the most part, I have tried not to chase money for, deep down, I've always been looked after.

I've learnt that vocation is also dynamic and of this moment. It grows and shifts as we learn and build on our experience. Being close to God and trying to help others remain a priority after all these years. It's been a bumpy road due to my careless driving with many diversions and distractions! However, I did get to do some work in Africa thanks to Pauline, and my latest book, '*Prayer is not what you think*," is about to be published. I wonder what Fr Ford would think of it.

For me, vocation is a lifelong journey made up of two elements - a journey (outwards) to others and a journey (inwards) to our inner selves. Both 'dual aspects' of vocation intersect, overlap, and become one in all that we are as we journey with others. This is where vocation finds its common purpose in all of us together. For our ultimate vocation is to become love, spread love, and build love as one.

Our past informs who we are today and today presents us with all that we must do. It's a personal calling to move forward with all that we have learnt over the years, all the skills, knowledge, and experience that we've picked up, and all the wonderful people that we've met.

All that we experience today is a gift for us to take forward in new ways as we continue to become all that we are intended to be. So, follow your vocation each day, outwards and inwards. Sit in silence, help others, do the work that matters, be grateful, and maybe... write your diary. It would be great to hear your story. Take care, Des

Day 200 – Vocational Guidance

Be gracious.
Be kind.
Listen.
Ask questions.
Smile.

Be positive,
no matter what.
Find the good in every situation.
Search for alternatives,
even if you cannot see any.

Do not boast.
Do not take the credit.
Be humble.
After all, your success
is because of others.

Recognise that you are not perfect,
and that this in itself is perfect.
Accept that others are not perfect,
and that is the way
it is meant to be.

You do not have to know everything.
Just work with those you can help
and with others who can help you.
Love plays to people's strengths.
Discover and celebrate the talents of others.

Your workplace is the whole world.
Your task is to reach out to all,
for you are responsible for everyone.
This is not an impossible task.
It is your gift of compassion to those in need.

Be ambitious
for all that you can be.
Remember that you can
achieve absolutely anything,
with the right support.

Surprise others.
Make them laugh.
Do the unexpected.
Make every day different
and every meeting memorable.
Make every customer
feel amazing with your smile.

Respond to unhelpful people with kindness.
Answer aggression with politeness.
Stick to your own framework of love
no matter what difficulties arise.
For all things will pass.

Stay young
no matter how old you are.
Be wise and listen
no matter how young you are.
Always.

What you do today is your legacy.
Use every moment.
Explore.
Wonder at the sunrise, the water
and the smile of the child.

Embrace those you love
every day.
Hug them and tell them
that they are truly amazing.
Tell them you love them.

Your children
will teach you everything
you need to know.
Your grandchildren
will teach you even more.

Remember that you are working
in every minute.
And being rewarded
with the gift of life.
Never work for just money,
for time is so precious.

Every person is a star.
Every conversation an inspiration.
Capture value from everything,
for it has all been given to you as a gift.
Be thankful.

Your work is you.
It isn't an office building or a factory.
Take your work into every situation,
as a force for good,
as a champion of kindness.

You are a fountain of love.
You can choose
to be majestic
or to keep your tap turned off.
You are the fountain of all love.

All love can flow through you.
All the love that has ever been
and ever will be,
is connected to you,
and through you.

Your health will not always be good
so never take it for granted.
Waking up in the morning
is the most amazing gift ever,
for one day, it will cease.

Be bold.
Be brave.
Be daring.
Be adventurous. Be creative.
For love

Shake the tree and rattle the cage.
How else will you know if
apples will fall or if lions will roar?
Then gather the apples
and open the cage.

Don't accept half measures.
Don't settle for anything less than brilliant.
Bring out the best in everyone.
For if it is worth doing,
it's worth doing right.

Don't be self-sufficient!
Build amazing relationships every day
with your partner, your family,
your community,
and your many workplaces.

Decide where you're going.
Imagine all that you should be.
Focus on this each day.
Don't get distracted.
Stay your course and claim that prize.

Just because it hasn't been done before
doesn't mean you can't do it.
Just because everyone else has failed
doesn't mean you will.
Just because others say something
doesn't mean it's true.
Listen to yourself.

Go for a walk
on your own
every day.
Sit in silence and
try not to think.

Forgive yourself.
Always.
Stop beating yourself up.
You are perfect as you are.
You have nothing to prove to anyone.

Be thankful every single night.
Recognise all that has happened
and the fact that you were part of all
that has happened today.
You played your part in
the theatre of the world.

Sometimes it's good to
act fast.
Other times it's good to sit and
do nothing.
Go with the flow.

You are not on your own.
You are not alone,
even in your darkest moments.
All times will pass.
And love will continue to grow

Be successful before 10 o'clock each day.

Always say yes.
Ask for help, for it's a sign of strength.
Build linkages,
and enable others to play their part.
Be enthusiastic in your work,
and smile.

You are amazing!
Use your voice and
say what is important to you.
Decide on your purpose
and play every day
with possibilities.

PERSONAL DEVELOPMENT EXERCISE

1. Begin your daily diary of writing today.

2. Choose an 'Inverted Pyramid Exercise' each day

About the Author

Des McCabe is one of the leading experts on inclusion and personal development. His latest books include 'The Inverted Pyramid of Inclusion: A Personal Invitation from Pope Francis' and his acclaimed series of 'Inverted Pyramid Exercises: 200 Personal Development Reflections (Vol 1-3).'

In the early part of his career, Des founded TBG, which grew to become the largest independent training organization in the UK. When the company was sold in 1995, it was finding jobs for 5,000 long-term unemployed and helping 4,000 people to get qualifications every year.

Des's expertise in the field of job creation led to him becoming an advisor to the British, Irish, US, Argentinian, Romanian, and Albanian governments on employment and inclusion. He received formal recognition as one of the leading job-creation entrepreneurs from 'Europe's 500,' Europe's most prominent body of entrepreneurs.

Des served as Chair of the European Union's cross-border Interreg training group in Northern Ireland and as Chair of the EU Border Training Bureau. He was an advisor to the Irish and US Governments in the early stages of the Northern Ireland Peace Process and went on to design the 'Peace Builder' training programme with US Special Envoy Senator George Mitchell's Northern Ireland Fund for Reconciliation.

Beyond his professional achievements, Des established and raised funding for The Training Trust, an international charity set up to meet the humanitarian needs of children in Romanian orphanages. He has assisted with Comic Relief projects in Kenya and supported a range of anti-poverty initiatives in Ghana and Madagascar.

In 2003 Des founded Diversiton as a social enterprise. The Inclusion Calendar is used internationally by hundreds of organisations. The annual International Inclusion Awards and The Diversity Champion Awards are also administered by Diversiton.

As a Coach, Des is well known for his experience in licensing, helping many colleagues to license their training courses and services across the world.

In 2011, Hay House published Des McCabe's ground-breaking book 'Work It Out!: How to Find the Work You Always Wanted in a Shifting Jobs Market' which led to the development of the Inverted Pyramid methodology.

From 2015, the Irish Government and numerous Agencies supported a wide range of Inverted Pyramid pilot initiatives to build inclusion in communities and workplaces. Inverted Pyramid training licenses became available worldwide for individuals, organisations, and government agencies in 2023. Des continues to support all of this.

Connect with Des:

VISIT - www.desmccabe.com / www.invertedpyramid.info
CONTACT - diversiton@gmail.com / +44 7717 203325

My Experience with The Asylum Process

By Faith Gakanje-Ajala

Like many refugees from across the world who live in the United Kingdom today, I harbored the hope of returning to Zimbabwe within my first six months as long as the risk to my personal safety was removed. Unfortunately, this did not happen, and even though I was no longer in Zimbabwe, I continued to live in fear. On several occasions, I received threatening telephone calls from 'men in dark glasses,' secret agencies. I felt as though I was constantly under surveillance. I did not feel free to move about as I wished. I also found it hard to trust people with my telephone number and other personal information. This forced me to apply to normalize my stay in the United Kingdom. I made an application for asylum in December 2002.

Self-Healing (Wellness is a Choice)

It took almost eight years for my asylum application to be processed and upheld. What a far cry from the rhetoric published in Home Office policy documents! The Home Office has widely publicized its target to make decisions on 98% of *straightforward asylum claims within six months.* Readers should note the loaded wording used by the Home Office to define this service standard. Using the term 'straightforward asylum claims,' they can easily fudge the statistics and disguise the system's poor performance as a failure to find candidates that meet the right criteria. Any claim which is not processed within six months can be simply dismissed as 'complex' and not 'straightforward.' The absence of a definition of a straightforward asylum claim makes it easy to disguise poor performance and injustice to asylum seekers.

Interestingly, an investigation carried out by the chief inspector of borders and immigration found that among the 'non-straightforward' asylum cases, over 50% of all cases handled by the Home Office, a significant number of these claims should never have been categorized as *not straightforward.* There was nothing 'complex' about my case. I was a vulnerable woman facing the real risk of persecution. Upon reflection, I still cannot understand why it took almost a decade to process and uphold my application. My application was rejected four times before it was finally upheld on the fifth attempt. Each time I turned up for an interview or hearing, I encountered a different team with very little knowledge of my case. I found myself repeating myself, outlining the same story time over and over again.

I had a valid case, but the authorities did not believe me. There were times when I was deprived of the help and support that I needed to at least present my case effectively. Initially, I was provided with legal support, but this aid ceased after the second dismissal of my application. After this, I had to turn to the voluntary sector and private individuals to assist with legal support. For my first interview, I also had the support of an interpreter. After that, they withdrew that support as they claimed my level of English was 'adequate.' This was far from the case. I still felt I needed this type of support as a lot of what was said in many of these interviews went over my head. English is indeed one of the official languages in Zimbabwe. However, this does not mean every Zimbabwean has mastery of it. Fluency and competence in English largely depend on one's level of education and age. In my case, my mother tongue is Shona. People from my region who speak some form of decent English speak a variant of English blended with our indigenous languages. My knowledge of the English language was basic, and I did not feel well-equipped to present my case.

The struggle that I went through in trying to plead my case and being dismissed simply because of a barrier in language that could be easily mediated with assistance served as the foundation of my understanding of the world. Withholding basic care, service, and consideration for someone in my situation should be considered a mild form of violence that inflicts deep wounds on the victim, wounds that I had to heal myself from amidst the English classes I had to take to improve my oratory skills.

The caseworkers at the Home Office failed to assess my claim fairly and sympathetically. Sometimes, it felt as though they had already decided my claim before the actual hearing. I didn't feel respected or listened to. I recall one occasion when I appeared before the tribunal panel on the day of my father's burial in Zimbabwe, which I couldn't attend. I was sobbing uncontrollably because of that, but the authorities misconstrued my tears and rejected my asylum claim, thinking it was an attempt to influence their decision. They finally suspended my legal aid. For that reason, I was classified as an illegal person from that time on. Adding to my challenges of being a foreign Black woman, withholding legal aid was a major setback I had not anticipated.

The members of staff were not trained to understand our Shona cultural practices. This invariably resulted in unfair decisions being made. The experience of going to court or to a meeting to represent myself was alien to me. Until recently, women were not allowed to represent themselves in my culture. This was done for them by their husbands or a male figure with social standing. For example, if my mum had a problem with a neighbor and this resulted in court action or an official complaint to the authorities, it would be my father's responsibility to deal with the issue on her behalf, hence the expression *kurova mukadzi wemunhu isimba kaviri*, a proverb that means if you beat someone's wife you should be prepared for a big fight with the husband. In the 1970s, girls were not allowed to go to school. Women's rights were often abused. They had difficulties getting identification cards, obtaining credit, and getting well-paid jobs. As a chief, my father broke the norm by empowering my sisters and me. We were allowed and encouraged to obtain an education, an empowerment that planted the seeds of spiritual and mental strength, which became critical for my future self-healing.

Self-Forgiveness: Not Needing Others' Forgiveness

The British government did not accommodate different cultural norms. In my culture, when we speak to people in authority, we do not look at them in the face, as this is a sign of respect. This is very different from the UK norm, where you are expected to look into people's eyes during conversations or interviews. Sometimes, I lost my appeals because I did not look the interviewer in the eye. The Home Office staff interpreted my tendency to look down or away from them during my interviews as a sign that I was providing them with false information.

Each time my case was rejected, my life became harder. Once my status changed to 'failed asylum seeker,' I lost entitlement to money to support me and all other support forms, including housing. I was expected to return home voluntarily or face forcible deportation after my second failed asylum claim. Once my benefits were withdrawn, I lived in abject poverty. As an asylum seeker, I had previously received a weekly allowance of £37.75 while my claim was being considered. I was also provided with housing. The allowance was paid in vouchers which could only be redeemed in designated outlets.

It works out at a little over £5 per day. It was an insult to live on this paltry sum. I could not afford to buy my traditional food. As far as possible, I had to content myself with potatoes and other food, which was not always welcome on my palate. Although African food is widely available in Nottingham, this is very expensive compared to locally produced food. I had to walk everywhere and rely on food aid and clothing banks to meet my basic needs. The food from the food banks was not always suitable. It was used food, which in most cases had passed the expiry or best-before date. I know someone who nearly died from food poisoning after she had eaten food from a corroded can that had passed its 'use by' date.

Perhaps the most serious problem of being a 'failed asylum seeker' was the loss of accommodation. My support from the National Asylum Service ended the moment my asylum claim was rejected. My landlord could no longer accommodate me, and I was automatically forced into the street. I was made homeless seven times. The first time this happened to me, I did not know what to do or who to turn to for help as I hardly knew anyone in the United Kingdom. I was picked up by a certain elderly lady while roaming the street in desperation for accommodation. This woman, who was riding a scooter, stopped and asked me why I was crying. I told her I felt lost and helpless. She was moved to tears when she learned I was thrown out of my accommodation. She offered me temporary shelter at her home.

On another occasion when I became homeless, I took up shelter for six months in a dilapidated building in Station Street, Nottingham, where the old police station was based before it moved to North Sherwood

Street. The building was infested with rats and cockroaches. It had no running water, heating, or furniture. I didn't even have a bed. Whenever the opportunity arose, I would take a bath or shower in other people's homes. More often than not, I had to settle for 'a top and tail' in a bucket with water. Despite the poor condition of the building, it held special meaning to me. It is the place where I buried my umbilical cord, much like the soil that holds the roots of a tree. The building is where I decided to take back my power.

Forgiveness was the first thing I had to do, not just to the people that could have helped but chose not to. I had to forgive myself for taking the blame for a wound I did not inflict and living in self-pity. I realized that the variation in my culture and the British made it difficult for them to understand that *kudya chemuzvere, hubata mwana.* This is a Shona proverb that translates to "*If you want to eat any food prepared by a mother of a newborn child, you have to hold the baby first.*" The proverb simply means that if you do not take care of the primary needs of those in your care, do not expect them to be at their best or be able to give you their best. Even if you do something small for them, it may go a long way in relieving their anxiety or lightening their burden and yours. So I decided to lighten my burden through forgiveness for the small gestures of service that the Asylum System withheld from me. Self-healing is a choice I made. I was done being a victim of circumstances, people, and myself. I wanted to heal and truly live.

Self-Responsibility: Not Blaming Others

One of the problems of homelessness and frequent address changes is the abuse of your data. If important letters with your personal details end up in the wrong hands, this can result in identity theft and other fraudulent activities. Although no one wants to take on the identity of an asylum seeker, this does not stop criminals from using your information to obtain credit. This was exactly what happened to me. Someone used my data to buy £1,200 worth of goods in Littlewoods. I faced immense difficulties in proving my innocence. After a lengthy investigation, my name was finally cleared. I attribute problems like this to the policies of the Home Office. Frequent re-housing of asylum seekers and withdrawal of their accommodation creates the conditions for a breach of asylum claimants' data rights. The Home Office owes asylum seekers and refugees a duty of care to handle their personal information in line with the provisions of the Data Protection Act. I know many asylum seekers and refugees who have had similar experiences to mine. Many have missed Home Office appointments, as letters about meetings have got lost or sent to the wrong address. They do not seem to have proper systems to track claimants' up-to-date addresses.

The Home Office needs to recognize that asylum-seekers with failed applications have the same needs as those whose applications are under consideration. They also need food, clothing, shelter, healthcare, and other services to meet their basic needs. There needs to be equality of service. The person is a human being with rights to fundamental services regardless of their status. Everyone should be given access to these basic services regardless of the outcome of their asylum application. It is this failure that has led some failed asylum-seekers to abscond, work in the so-called 'black economy,' and engage in illegal activities.

It was difficult to comprehend why the government would treat asylum-seekers in such an inhumane way. However, I have come to understand from public commentaries that keeping people in destitution is a key strand of the government's policy to force asylum-seekers to leave the country and to discourage others from seeking asylum in the United Kingdom. Rt Hon Iain Duncan Smith MP Preface to *Restoring Trust in the UK Asylum System*, The Centre for Social Justice: Asylum and Destitution Working Group, December 2008 argues that 'It also appears that the British government is using forced destitution as a means of encouraging people to leave voluntarily.'

In the report, Dr. Chris McDowell further observes, 'The asylum system has developed into a process that is more about controlling numbers than deciding who needs protection.' The reader should note that the government's policy of hostility takes several different forms. Among other things, this is reflected in its' dispersal strategy' whereby asylum seekers are not given a voice in where they live or the paltry amount of money allocated for their subsistence; in the inept approach to processing asylum applications; in exclusion from labor market participation; in social isolation; in the frequent reporting regime at regional reporting centers; and in the propensity to detain certain categories of asylum seekers.

Detaining asylum seekers for long periods is another strategy that was being used by the Home Office. While I was fortunate enough to avoid detention, I have some experience visiting other brothers and sisters who have been placed for long periods in detention centers; as part of my NAWEF remit, I have actively supported women who were in and out of detention centers. I was instrumental in championing the cause of asylum seekers even though, at the time, I had not yet gained refugee status.

It has now become clear that Home Office staff are driven by meeting targets – ticking boxes rather than listening properly to asylum seekers' stories in order to make a right, fair and informed decision. This was confirmed by a former caseworker in an anonymous public letter to *The Guardian* (8 April 2017) quoting an anonymous Home Office caseworker who said, 'I worry asylum caseworkers are failing people in their darkest hour… At the Home Office we're molded to be skeptical and work to unrealistic targets. Doing the right thing can mean taking a performance hit.'

In a more recent disclosure to journalists from *The Guardian*, three former Home Office caseworkers shed further light on the problems inherent in the asylum process. They described the asylum process as a 'lottery.' We are told that asylum interviews are 'rushed,' 'biased,' and 'intimidatory,' and the outcome often takes the form of 'copy and paste' decisions from previous cases. The starting position is that asylum seekers are 'liars.' As one whistle-blower put it: 'an attitude of cynicism towards asylum seekers became "a part of you"' (*The Guardian*, 11 February 2018).

This perception influences the way Home Office staff approach their work. Some caseworkers take pleasure in rejecting application claims without weighing up the evidence to judge the merit of the claim. Decisions are not always objective. It sometimes boils down to which caseworker was allocated to your case and their mood at a given point in time. Someone remarked that the way the Home Office handles cases of asylum seekers is like a lottery because if you've got a caseworker who is particularly refusal-minded and is determined to catch you out, then you're going to have a hard time. Inside information revealed that some enthusiasts have a reputation for never granting anything and seem to take pride in that. Significantly, the whistle-blowers also drew attention to issues relating to poor training for their roles, overwork, and the drawbacks of a target-driven culture. Staff is set an annual target of processing 225 claims or decision reports, which many find to be unrealistic. One whistle-blower described the challenge as follows: 'It affects the quality of the decisions… By the time you have been through the photos, the file, the news reports, it's three o'clock, and then you have to draft a report, a decision on someone's claim, which can often be more than 20 pages long, which is difficult to complete in two hours. Another whistle-blower complained about a lack of time to prepare for interviews. They shared with reporters that sometimes one does not get the file before the interview, so one does not know what the case is about. As a result, when you get into the interview, you start making on-the-spot inquiries. You start asking open-ended questions like: *'Can you tell me why you left X?'* This tends to embarrass the case workers.

Self-Resilience: The Ultimate Goal

"Destiny can only be delayed, never denied"

- Raymond Mahlalela

Real power lies in true leadership but the foundation of that power lies in self-leadership and good self-representation. The story of our lives can be healing to us if we live to tell it.

The ideas for many of the social projects which I subsequently launched came to me while I was living in that unsanitary, substandard building on Station St. in Nottingham. With the help of a good friend, Dianne Skerritt, I spent many sleepless nights working on my business plan and writing bids. This was the early beginning of the Nottingham African Women's Empowerment Forum (NAWEF). The whistle-blowers' disclosure brought back echoes of former Home Secretary John Reid's remarks in 2006 that the Home Office was *not fit for purpose.* He said to members of the Home Affairs Select Committee, 'Our system is not fit for purpose. It is inadequate in terms of its scope; it is inadequate in terms of its information technology, leadership, management systems, and processes.'

Following this damning assessment, the Department was restructured, and a more streamlined asylum process was introduced in March 2007, known as the New Asylum Model. At the time when the New Asylum Model was introduced, there was a huge backlog of cases. This was estimated at up to 450,000. A target was set by the Home Secretary for this to be cleared within 5 years. Willman and Knafler (*Support for Asylum-Seekers and Other Migrants: A Guide to Legal and Welfare Rights.* London, Legal Action Group, 2009) note that 'Part of the backlog was cleared by

UKBA issuing legacy questionnaires to individuals, many of whom had been waiting for an initial decision for more than three years.'

Significantly, I noticed a change in the culture after these changes were introduced. I began to see a glimpse of light at the end of the tunnel. There was a welcome improvement in the way my case was handled. I saw greater continuity in the personnel who were tasked with processing my application. A far greater effort was now made to listen to interviewees. The interviews felt less threatening. For the first time, I felt as though they were ready to genuinely understand my case and what would happen to me if I was forcibly deported back to Zimbabwe.

The richest wealth is wisdom.
The strongest weapon is Patience.
The best security is Faith.
The greatest tonic is Laughter,
and surprisingly all are free
and just make good use of all!

About the Author

Managing Director at Fagee Fashions

"From Humble Beginnings to a Powerhouse of Change: Faith's Incredible Journey to Empowering African Women in the UK

She may have been born into a large and humble family in Zimbabwe, but Faith's incredible journey has seen her rise to become a powerful force for change. The daughter of Chief Nemangwe and a proud mother of five children, Faith played a vital role in the 'Chimurenga', the Shona language word for liberation, of her homeland. From the age of 9 in the 70s, she was a Chimbwido, a junior freedom fighter.

Her early adult life was spent working as a community development officer and an activist in Zimbabwe. In 2002, she was forced to flee as a political refugee and migrate to the United Kingdom. In 2006, she founded the African Women's Empowerment Forum [AWEF], of which she is now a Director and CEO.

The AWEF organisation is an umbrella group that empowers African women migrants, refugees, women and children, those held in detention and asylum seekers, by providing advocacy and support to help them regain their freedom and fulfil their potential. Faith has also participated in the Migrants And Migration Impact Program, working across European countries advocating on issues of poverty and asylum.

In 2011, she led a national campaign to 'reunite me with my children' following legislation passed by the UK parliament to prevent migrants from uniting with their families. Faith is an active participant in the voluntary sector, serving as a philanthropist, volunteer, member of strategic boards. In 2022 she shadowed the Lord Mayor of Nottingham as part of her personal development, and in the same year became appointed as a city councillor in Nottingham.

Faith is a strategic planner, driven by effective outcomes, a member of Change-makers UK, and she has received numerous awards for her tireless social contributions nationally and internationally, including a business champion award in Zimbabwe in 1990, a UK Ryan foundation Fellowship award in 2010 and the TERN (The Entrepreneurial Refugee Network C.I.C.) Award in 2016.

Despite her socialist beliefs, Faith has also been successful in the business world, as an entrepreneur in the garment industry, running her own fashion house, Fagee Fashions & Enterprise. Faith honours her late father Mr. Mangisi Marumisa as the source of her inspiration and tireless work ethic. Faith is truly a visionary who has the ability to turn vision into reality.

Connect with Faith:

faith@awef.org.uk

www.awef.org.uk

www.LinkedIn.com/in/Faith-Gakanje-70352225/

How to Move Forward When You Feel Like You Are Out of Options

By Maria Dayton

Stepping out in faith

It is said that "There is no elevator to success, you have to take the stairs," —nowhere is this more apparent than if you are disabled and working at the US White House. There is no more ableist of an environment than the crumbling gray steps at the pinnacle of American power. The elevators rarely work, and the innumerable staircases spiral upwards w/no fluorescent marks, or handrails, or anything to distinguish them from the gray blobs I see from my diminished sight. These Darwinian obstacle courses are compounded by the rush and speed of everyday work - everything is late... everything is needed yesterday... the stairs are taken two at a time by young and agile staffers talking on two cell phones at the same time while texting and yelling orders to some unfortunate underling. There is a driving need to get things done before the midterm elections - fighting to stay on schedule—meeting visitors and escorting them through the snaking black and white and gray hallways before their 30 minutes are up. All I keep thinking is, "How will I ever survive here?" with my slowness, my fatness, my inability to distinguish the individual and nondescript stairs that seem to be a conduit to everything that matters.

My first day

I learned quickly that the security turnstiles are finicky at the White House—on my first day I got stuck inside a revolving door and experienced just enough side eye from the Secret Service and my colleagues to make me consciously speed up and smile nervously. There is a synchronized dance w/ security at the White House—entrances lock and seize up with a delicate pattern that if misjudged will bruise your thighs for days and incur wrath from busy staffers trying to avoid a pile up. You better move quickly and with the grace and ease afforded by your privileged rank and position. German Shepherd dogs pace and sniff at you in front of large industrial fans—as dresses blow and seconds are counted down with more precision than in any hostile frequent flier line at the airport.

As I pushed through the final freakishly heavy door—I was excited to look around the White House grounds and at my new life. As I walked towards my designated wing—I noticed the innumerable gray stairs flanking every building within eye sight—blurring out like pyramids before me. As someone who is visibly impaired—my heart sank as I scanned like Robocop for evidence of any alternative entry and exit points that could be accessed discretely and with a modicum of dignity. When my scanning came back w/ nothing—I knew that this would be a problem moving forward and I plotted my strategy of avoidance. I didn't want to ask my designated escorts where the handicapped accessible elevators were or where handicapped people existed in general—I felt the shame wash over me, along w/ a wave of insecurity and doubt. I hoped to God that I could fake my normalness and that no one would notice my perceived defects. This worked for a period of time.

My Fears Manifested

The life of a disabled person at the White House is one of deft misdirection. We have an abacus of available energy and we are constantly scanning for ways to manage our environment and to time our encounters w/ a precision that resembles Julia Child on a good day. My goal was to engage in walking conversations and then time urgent calls to a time just before my colleagues headed up the stairs. The goal was to re-emerge at a later time—with the perfect excuse and w/ a phone in-hand. This worked for day-to-day activities for a time, but I was ultimately bested by the inevitable White House photo ops that follow almost every meeting and those looming gray stairs that had bothered me from the beginning.

I tried my best to avoid these occasions—and to deflect and escape before the photographers emerged, but never fail, they always seemed to arrive before the normal work ended and they followed groups around w/ a tenacity that was hyenalike. The usual demand was for visiting delegations and staffers to line up on the outside stairs for a series of pictures. Despite my efforts, it was very difficult to avoid meetings that bled into corridors and continued into hallways—which made it almost impossible to avoid these stairs and the pictures that inevitably came afterwards. I hated these moments because I couldn't differentiate individual stairs and there were no railings to assist in the steep climbs and descents that had to be made while laughing and talking w/ colleagues and visiting dignitaries. I hated walking down corridors with visitors—knowing that it was just a matter of time before I needed to step out into the abyss and risk injury and humiliation for a photo that I would dislike and inevitably delete from my social media.

In these moments—as the corridors became shorter and shorter—and as the stairs and the outside emerged—my first inclination was to run down the long carpeted hallways and to escape from outside eyes. I was terrified that they would see my weakness and that I would lose whatever advantage I might have achieved despite my gender and class and weight. I was terrified that my vulnerability would mean an end to the respect that I had begrudgingly earned through years of hard work and that my colleagues would close ranks against me and anyone else who wasn't "normal" or who fell short of unspoken rules and rigid standards. Thankfully these White House photo ops forced me to confront these underlying and limiting assumptions about how people operate and I learned many valuable lessons over time about the power of leading with vulnerability.

What I Discovered

Once I determined that these forays onto the stairs were unavoidable, I began noticing that certain male colleagues would intuitively offer me their elbow as I approached the top of the stairs. (Many of these same colleagues I still work w/ today in varying other capacities.) This helped me understand that vulnerability isn't a weakness, but actually a strength, because it allowed people around me to show me their support in ways that were unexpected and surprising.

It also allowed me to filter and access the character of my circles and to ultimately surround myself with those who are compassionate and who had my best interest at heart. I learned that by stepping out in faith that my perceived weaknesses became my strength; and that the negative voices in my head were not only untrue but also counterproductive.

Final Takeaways

When you own your weaknesses and your vulnerabilities you allow people to surprise you by responding to your needs

If you step out in faith and in authenticity people around you will rise to the occasion

The narratives we tell ourselves about our limitations are often untrue - whether it be about class, race, gender, weight, disability etc

Vulnerability is an asset that can help assess character and realign social circles

---

"Owning our story can be hard but not nearly as difficult as spending our lives running from it. Embracing our vulnerabilities is risky but not nearly as dangerous as giving up on love and belonging and joy—the experiences that make us the most vulnerable. Only when we are brave enough to explore the darkness will we discover the infinite power of our light."

— Brene Brown

About the Author

"Until the lion has a voice,
every story will glorify the hunter."

African proverb

Maria Lynne Dayton is a successful social entrepreneur, systems architect, and creative finance expert who has developed, funded, and managed over 20 major development and IT projects on 4 continents ($140m) with a variety of stakeholders including: international organizations, governments, civil society, and the private sector. She specializes in achieving systemic impact at the nexus between capital, technology, and government.

Her current passion is the creative financing of the UN Sustainable Development Goals and last mile infrastructure; blending different approaches such as blockchain, impact investment, and crowd finance (Raised $140M in project financing / $10B in hybrid/blended capital deals). As a White House Presidential Innovation Fellow, she led "citizen experience" across 24 federal agencies—winning the 2019 Service to the Citizen Award; and as an Impact Fellow at Singularity University, she led several moonshot initiatives with a coalition of Fortune 50 companies and foundations around global health and small business finance. Currently she is the Director of Capital Partnerships at LG NOVA—the innovation arm of LG Electronics. While at LG she led their global Grand Challenges (1300+ startups) team and founded the LG Capital Alliance (40+ funds / $500 m in investments / 5 acquisitions). Recently she helped found the first venture capital and ESG funds in LG's history including the LG NOVA Prime Capital Fund - $100m, and the LG NOVA Growth Fund - $500m.

Maria has co-founded a number of companies, including Transterra Media, an award-winning online marketplace that is changing the way companies source news and marketing video. Transterra currently has offices in Dallas and London where it brokers and produces video stories (8000+) for large satellite broadcasters and brands (280+) that empower local voices. These stories have a reach of over a trillion globally with 70% of profits returning to local producers. Transterra has received awards from Red Herring, Wamda, The Dublin Web Summit, and was selected by Mashables as one of its *Top 25 Startups in Unlikely Places.* Our stories have received the following awards: 2 Oscars, 1 BAFTA, 13 World Press Photo first prizes, 2 Emmys, 2 Peabody awards, 1 Pulitzer, 4 Time Photo of the Year, and 2 National Geographic Annual Awards.

Maria holds a BA in International Studies and Biology from Gonzaga University, as well as, MAs from both France and Egypt in International Relations, International Economic Development, and Middle East Studies. She consults regularly with governments and IGOs on citizen engagement, alternative finance, and ecosystem development.

Connect with Maria:

maria@marialynnedayton.com

www.MariaLynneDayton.com

LinkedIn.com/in/MariaDayton

Road to Damascus

By Keith Trubshaw

Sign, or Lose it Anyway

I am lying on the hospital trolley. My leg is hurting; they've told me I need an operation. My feet have gone through the swing doors that lead to the operating theatre, my head is still outside. Someone comes along to stop my progress.

'You need to sign this, please,' he says, handing me a clipboard. I read through it.

'I'm not signing that,' I say.

'Why not?'

'Because you're going to take my leg off!'

'We are trying to save it, if you don't sign, we can't operate, and if we don't operate, you will lose it anyway.'

I signed.

I awoke from the operation on the morning of my 25th birthday.

'Please, God, let it be there.'

It was!

I had started my business just a few months before with not much ability, no orders in the pipeline, and very little money. But what I did have was a dream I was determined to pursue and an unshakeable belief that I would succeed. Unfortunately, I'd been crushed by several tons of steel which had fallen across my legs. As it turned out, that wasn't the only blow I suffered. The value of the steel represented everything I had in the business, almost to the penny. While I was in hospital, it was shipped to my customer, who promptly went bankrupt. But at least I still had two legs. Over the years, I have always maintained that business starts on a dream but so often ends on a nightmare. Mine could so easily have ended there and then. But we have only lost when we give up, right?

That incident wasn't the first blow I suffered in my life, and it certainly proved not to be the last. For me, four decades of being in business have been a rollercoaster ride, basking in the glow of success before plunging into the depths of despair more times than I care to remember. However, there is a huge difference between a rollercoaster ride and being in business. On a rollercoaster, we endure the slow climb to the top so that we can enjoy the thrill of descent, but in business, it's very much the other way around. The thrill is in the climb, witnessing what we are trying to build take shape. But when we reach the top, whenever or wherever that may be, the descent is anything but thrilling. It can be a scary, often terrifying ride to despair. And yet when we have ridden that ride and travelled that journey more than once, surely we learn that at the bottom of the track, we can buy another ticket and start again if we wish. Some people say, '*Yes, I want another go*,' while others are too wounded and terrified to ever get off their knees. I guess I was one of those who got up and started all over again, not once but several times over the years. What things did I learn from those experiences? Well, first off, I learned that success is a great teacher, but failure is a far better one. That said, failure might well be a great teacher, but the teacher can only teach pupils who will listen. In my case, there were too many times that I didn't listen. If I didn't make the same mistakes, I found a new set to add to my repertoire of cock ups.

There are those we meet, whether in person, on a screen, or within the pages of a book, who have learned lessons and gained knowledge that they pass on to others. I don't feel that I'm one of those. I'm just a guy with a bloody nose. It seems that all my journey has taught me is that I have more questions than answers. I am just someone who has walked the path before and hopefully knows where the rocks and pitfalls lie in wait for the unwary. And yet, if we are on an unfamiliar path and the way before us is cast in shadow, I guess it's nice to know that someone has been there before and lived to tell the tale. Maybe that someone can shine a light, if not to guide us, at least show where the vicious rocks are lurking. What makes me so special that you should listen to my advice? Why should my so-called light that shines the way be any brighter than anyone else's? The answer is that it isn't... It's just another light, one of thousands competing for your attention, like fireflies on a dark night. All the lights will illuminate a better path; my light, such as it is, has been dulled by the battle scars it has suffered along the way.

I've been in business for most of my life, a serial entrepreneur finding my own way. Stumbling and falling more times than I care to remember but always managing to get up and carry on. Admittedly, sometimes it took me a long time to stagger to my knees, but I managed to do it in the end. Someone wrote that 'It's not how hard we hit the ground, it's how high we bounce afterwards.' Great words, indeed.

After that first catastrophe, I was faced with starting again. In hindsight, that was an easy decision as, truth be told, there was little alternative. How do we come back from devastating blows? Well, for me, even then, as with now, one of my most valuable assets, the thing I hold more precious than anything else, is integrity. I was philosophically innocent then (I probably still am), but even as a 25-year-old, I knew I had to take responsibility for what had happened. So I did just that and called all of my suppliers to tell them that I wouldn't be able to pay their bills when they fell due. Each and every one of them responded to my honesty by extending my credit to give me a chance to get back on my feet. By being honest, even though I delivered bad news, I improved my status in their eyes. It's so easy to blame others for our misfortune. Doing that does not serve us. Whatever the problem, take responsibility.

Perspective

Everything that happens in our lives, good or bad, makes us feel a certain way. Happy, sad, elated, maybe fearful? Wrong! It is not what has happened, what someone said or didn't say that gives rise to our feelings; it is our interpretation of those things. That interpretation is a matter of choice. Between everything that happens to us and our reaction to it, there is a space. A space in which we are free to decide what that reaction will be. Think about this, how many times have you heard someone say, '*You've made me angry*?' Indeed, how many times have we ourselves uttered such words? Here's the thing, it's not their words that made us angry; it is our interpretation of those words and then our decision to choose to be angry or sad, or simply ambivalent.

When something bad happens, or someone says cruel things, consider this; all of those comments and happenings are rocks that are thrown at us as we try to make our way through life. Some are delivered with malice or jealousy, while others might simply be unintentional or accidental, but all of them, without exception, serve to make us stronger. When you were born, your life stretched out in front of you on a smooth flat road, straight and true, not deviating a single inch from what would surely be a wonderful future. But then, as you grew, childhood friends were cruel to you; maybe your parents left you. Adulthood saw more hurtful things and cruel rocks thrown your way. Some missed their mark and fell to the ground around you; others stung you deeply before falling at your feet. Every single one of those rocks and stones that surround you was cast there to prevent your progress, to make your path more difficult.

Yet, what are rocks and stones when we view them from above, when we change our perspective? They are stepping stones that help us move forward, help us to grow. If our path has always been smooth and level, with not a rock in sight, and then suddenly that path points upwards, becoming a steep incline that we have to climb, if we lose our footing, we will fall back to the very bottom. But if that road is strewn with rocks and stones that have been cast our way in the past, then those rocks and stones become footholds. We are stronger; we may slip back a short distance but soon will regain our footing. I'm sure we can all think of times when we felt that the world was against us, that there was no way forward, and that the pain of all those stones striking us was just too great to bear. I promise you that if you fast-forward, you will see that life doesn't happen *to* you; it happens *for* you.

Maybe I should close this section by giving you an example that's very personal to me. When I was 11 years old, I waved goodbye to my father for the last time. He was killed in a car accident later that day. My mother was left with three children and took on three cleaning jobs to make ends meet. But what happened to the youngest child? As I grew into adulthood, there was no dad to help me fix things, show me how to use tools, or take me to the football the way that dads do. I had to find my own way. I am not giving you a sob story...far from it.

Now, as I look back, I realise that by no longer being around, dad gave me a great gift. He forged my independence, my ability to stand on my own two feet. As I said… life doesn't happen *to* us; it happens *for* us!

Faith

Over the years, there were countless occasions when different members of my staff (we called them staff in those days. Nowadays, it's more fashionable to replace the words 'staff' or 'employees' with 'team'. I can't help noticing that the ones who are most vocal in that regard are so often the ones who treat their staff as anything but a team. But that's the subject of another book.) came to me questioning my judgement. Things like… *I don't think I can do that. That can't be done! What makes you think that will work?* My answer was invariably the same… *Because I've got faith!* This wasn't faith in the religious sense, though for many, that doubtless has its place, but faith that situations will work out for the best.

Years ago, before the law of attraction had come so much to the fore, I used to call it the *law of expectation.* If I expected something to work out, genuinely expected it to work out as opposed to just hoping it would work out, it usually did.

Since those days, I've discovered that my use of the term *expectation* in that regard was not original. It was being spoken of by the late great Neville Goddard, whose wise and uncomplicated teachings can still be found on the Internet.

So there it is; things always worked out when I had faith that they would.

But what gives us this faith? What distinguishes it from blind hope and wishful thinking? For me, it's being able to see things from the end. Imagining what things will be like when something is completed, with no doubt whatsoever that it will come to pass. However, there's a big caveat here. Having faith is not enough on its own. Those who regale us with the assurance that all we have to do is *imagine* for something to come to pass are selling us short. We have to work. Maybe we don't have to work excessively hard, but we can't just sit on our backside; we have to put ourselves in a position to receive. Otherwise, it's like being offered a gift but refusing to hold out our hand to receive it. If you don't want to do the work, then all of the good fortune that lives on the other side of that vivid imagination of yours will have gone to waste.

Smilers Win

The world is full of people who believe beyond all doubt that once they are successful, happiness will follow. They have so much in common with the people centuries ago who believed that the Sun revolved around the Earth. They were amazed when Copernicus proved it was the other way around, and all this time, it was mother earth who had been dancing her yearly dance around the Sun. How often do we hear things like… '*When I have that car, or once I have all of that money, I will be happy.*' Time and time again, it has been shown that success does not lead to happiness. It is the other way around. The happier you are, the more successful you are likely to be.

Across almost five decades since I started in business, the biggest mistake I made was this – I forgot to take my happiness along with me. I discarded it in the pursuit of money. Oh yes, I knew the teaching that money is the root of all evil, that the pursuit of money for its own sake is not the way to go. But I thought I was the exception. I thought that my happiness lay at the end of a financial rainbow. How wrong I was.

A few years ago, I retired. My pension investment was so good that there was no need for me to work ever again. That retirement was just two months old when suddenly the money was gone. All of it! The company to whom I'd entrusted a lifetime worth of pension contributions had been raided by the police amid accusations of it being a Ponzi scheme. I was broke, and I mean broke! I couldn't pay my mortgage, I couldn't put fuel in my car. I was angry, hurt, and at the bottom of nowhere to go. But deep down, I knew that it was my own fault. There are three things that are easy to rip off in this world, ambition, bereavement, and greed. I fell full square into the last category. I should've heeded the warning voices, but I thought I knew better. I lost every penny.

Aeroplanes and Potatoes

Over the years, I'd had yachts and aeroplanes, all the trappings of a rich man. Now I was reduced to riding on an old rusty bicycle as the only way to get around. On one occasion, I was riding home along a quiet country lane when I spotted a potato that had been spilt from a farm trailer. I stopped and looked around because I was ashamed, yet, I picked it up. It would be my dinner that day. Looking back, that moment of shame was when my life turned around. It gave me something which had long since deserted me; the gift of humility and the realisation that happiness is a decision. I realised that all of those trappings meant nothing. Then and there, I decided to be happy. I allowed my hands, so long clenched into fists for fear of losing what I had, to open up, to allow them to act as a cup sitting in the flow of life. Everything changed.

Nicola's Story

I was on my way to Glasgow but had to call in to see a client in Liverpool on the way. I had to park my car on a side street some distance away from his office. Getting out, I noticed a girl sitting in a doorway on the far side of the road. As I walked to the parking pay point, she asked me if I had any spare change.

'No, sorry,' I replied. But having paid my parking fee, I was left with just a small amount of change. I crossed the road to give it to her. I am always reminded of Mother Theresa's words in these situations where she challenged us to help someone feel they are not alone. As I gave her the money, I bent down to speak with her.

'Why are you here?' I asked. 'This street is really quiet.'

'I'm ashamed,' she said. 'I don't want people to know I've come to this.'

She told me that she was trying to get the money together to buy some clean underwear. As she spoke, a single tear flowed down her cheek; that tear moved me deeply. She wasn't begging because it was easy money; she had nowhere to go and no one to turn to.

As I lay in my hotel room that night, pondering the important meetings I'd had that day, it suddenly hit me that they mattered, not a jot. The most important one by far was that one in a doorway. It changed my life. No one should have to face what that girl faced. All it would take would be for people to care a little more, for people like her not to be alone—to be warm and know that someone is there for them.

Her name was Nicola. I hope you are warm and safe and happy, Nicola. I should have done more; we all should.

The moral of the story? For all of us who seek to do well, just remember that money is just *do good tokens*. If we all saw it as that, the world would be a better, kinder place. A place where we can be happy and content to leave our children when it's time for us to move on.

About the Author

Described as a serial entrepreneur Keith set up his first enterprise whilst still at school. By his late twenties, he'd established a successful business, growing exponentially against a tide of recession. Other businesses followed with varying degrees of success (and failure). He maintains that all of them brought lessons, some learned at the time, others only after years of hindsight. Nowadays, as the CEO of a successful consulting company, his enthusiasm for business and, indeed, life is undiminished.

As well as an entrepreneur and writer, Keith is an accomplished musician, the chairman of a local football club, and gives his time to his old school to show the youngsters (as he puts it) ... 'If an idiot like me can do it, so can you'. He has two sons and lives with his incredibly tolerant wife in Shropshire, England.

Connect with Keith:

keith@thelonelyseat.com

www.TheLonelySeat.com

www.LinkedIn.com/in/Keith-Trubshaw-854b77551/

Healing Naturally, An "Unconventional" Journey to Health

By Naomi Watson

It is a cold morning in February 2007. I am lying on a hard bed, looking up at the ceiling. I am in a small room with a window; although the sun is shining, it is cold. I can smell that distinctive smell in that one place, the scent of fear.

I can hear faint voices outside, the sound of people rushing, and the bleeping of equipment behind me. I can also hear the sounds that say so much without saying anything.

My thoughts seem to wander; I am thinking of what I would ask him. I had been asked to change and wait for him. I am cold in the thin gown that has been handed to me. I wonder how long he is going to be.

The door opened, and the oncologist went straight to his table and chair. He spoke to Malcolm, my husband, about what would happen next. He talks about chemotherapy and radiotherapy. I listen and am a bit upset that I don't seem part of the conversation. I ask, "Why am I lying here? Can I get dressed now?" He stands up, hesitates, and comes to me. He checked the wound and said I had healed well and could get dressed. I was diagnosed with breast cancer on January 4th, 2007. It was Grade 3, ductal, invasive, aggressive breast cancer. This was an appointment with the oncologist for the next step of the treatment.

I get dressed and go to a chair near him. I said, "I don't want to take chemotherapy yet. I am going to try some natural therapies and then decide." He gets up, throws my file on the table, and says to me in a raised voice, "I know people like you who go for alternative therapies and return when it's too late to do anything." I am stunned. There was no discussion, no finding out what I meant or wanted to do, what I understood, or if I had any questions. My mind goes blank. I say to myself, *I will not come here even if I am on my deathbed.*

He then continued to tell me that I should be grateful, that it cost the NHS £17k, and I was refusing the treatment. I replied, "Well, I am saving the NHS from spending the amount." He was not too pleased with my response.

I had come to ask if I could postpone my therapies by just one month to go to the States, go through the Natural Recovery Programme I had researched, and then decide about chemotherapy and radiotherapy. After my altercation, I knew I didn't want to take the chemo. It was probably my stubborn streak, and I didn't consider the consequences. The doctor then went on to say that having the chemo now was essential. I couldn't postpone it. Once you are in the system and a plan has been set, it is almost like you have no choice; you need to keep going, no questions asked after the doctor has decided.

I came away from that appointment determined that there had to be another way. I was not going to be bullied into something I didn't want. As the consultant had rightly said as we got up to go - it's my body, and it will be my decision, and I will have to live with the consequences of my decision.

Discovering Simple Remedies that Heal

You cannot control what happens to you, but you can control your attitude towards what happens to you, and in that, you will be mastering change rather than allowing it to master you.

\- Brian Tracy

As soon as the surgical wound after the mastectomy healed, I went to Uchee Pines Institute, United States of America, for a whole 'natural rational therapies' programme. This wasn't as life-changing as I had expected. There were new therapies I was introduced to - hydrotherapy, oxygen therapy, special teas, and sunbathing. I was already following (although not strictly) all the other therapy elements of the programme. The lifestyle we practise is simple but not easy to implement because of our cultivated habits! It all sounded pretty simple, and I was determined that this was the time to learn and implement.

My ultimate goal was to learn everything I could and put into practice all that was required of me over the 17-day recovery programme and be in good health. The programme included nutrition, exercise, and various other therapies.

1. Nutrition is integral to healing - Let food be your medicine!

Although I came prepared to face anything to succeed (or so I thought), by the third morning of seeing salad on my plate, I felt uneasy… I just felt sick… unable to face another 'salad' for breakfast! Well, it's not just salad but the six cloves of garlic that came with it. Later that morning, I told my doctor that I couldn't face salad for breakfast. He looked at me, smiled, and said it was my choice and I didn't have to have it. He said I could go back to it when I was ready, which meant there was no other option apart from the salad!

I reminded myself that choices have consequences. The thought of eating steamed garlic on its own made me change my attitude. I 'treated' myself to 'garlic sandwiches.' Take two thick slices of tomato and add the sliced garlic in between, smile, and finish the breakfast….

This was just the beginning of my favourite way to think differently about presenting and eating. That would be my 'mantra' for eating. Is what I am about to eat, or required to eat, going to feed my good cells or my bad (cancer) cells? If it will feed my good cells, how do I learn to love what I have to eat? If it feeds my bad cells, how do I avoid what I should not eat or learn better alternatives for my good cells?

The menu for breakfast and lunch would be 'salad.' I was encouraged to eat just two meals. This would mean I would be 'fasting' for more hours than I was used to, from lunchtime to the following breakfast.

I am not a big eater, and salad takes so much chewing that I wasn't eating much. By the evening, I felt faint with no energy, so the doctor suggested eating some salad for supper. The only addition was a glass of carrot juice and aloe vera before lunch.

I soon set goals of learning to 'enjoy' these salads without any dressings at first. After a few days, we could add beans and other cooked foods, but I persevered because I struggled to eat the salads. I decided that if the raw salads were good for me, I would have them for 17 days to get into the good habit of eating and enjoying salads.

The salad was colourful, raw, and varied. As days passed, my attitude changed. I learnt to appreciate the tastes of different items and their usefulness. There were various greens, tomatoes, cucumber, chopped herbs, broccoli, courgettes, and celery. I soon learnt that our diet consisted of only plant foods. Plant foods provide immune-boosting and cancer-fighting substances, beginning with the antioxidant vitamins C, E, and beta-carotene. Also, plant foods provide a broad spectrum of vitamins, minerals, and other health-promoting substances. Only plants contain potent substances called phytochemicals, which scientists are now discovering protect us from cancer, heart disease, and an array of other serious illnesses.

Plants are also the primary source of all minerals in the diet. Fibre is an essential substance that protects us from cancer, especially cancers of the large intestine and breast. Plants are the only source of fibre, which binds in our intestines with fat, cholesterol, environmental pollutants, and disease-causing hormones, and eliminates these dangers from the body.

2. Fasting Heals

As I learnt to enjoy salad, I was also introduced to fasting. Learning about it and witnessing some benefits sealed the importance of fasting.

Fasting, one of the oldest therapies in medicine, is staying away from all foods and drinks for a short or long period. It plays an essential role in cultural and religious practices in one form or another. It can take the form of complete abstinence or a lighter or lower-calorie form of eating.

It can be eating raw food for the day or drinking vegetable juices. Intermittent fasting is a dietary practice that alternates between periods of eating and not eating. Unlike other diets that focus on *what* to eat, intermittent fasting focuses on *when* to eat.

My two meals a day took into account what I ate and when I ate it and helped boost my immune system.

3. Water Heals

I was required to drink four litres of water every day. I could manage two litres, but struggled to drink more than that. I had to build up the quantity of water slowly. Learning the unique benefits of water and its healing properties, I understood why water is deemed a fundamental human right.

Cleanse - Water is the best liquid to cleanse tissues. Drinking sufficient water helps supply the system's necessities and assists nature in resisting disease. Simple, pure water to drink and fresh air to breathe invigorates the vital organs, purifies the blood, and helps the heart overcome the dire conditions of the system.

The four litres of water included some herb teas.

- Four cups of Pau d'arco tea daily (the tea is made by boiling four teaspoons of the herb in four cups of water for 15 minutes, then steeping for 15 minutes more).
- 2-4 cups of chaparral tea daily
- Blue-violet and red clover tea

Although hydrating the body with drinking water and herb teas was helpful, the other water use was **Hydrotherapy treatments.**

One of the daily treatments was the 'fever treatment' or hydrotherapy treatment. Also referred to as water cure, it is part of naturopathy that involves water for pain relief and treatment. It stimulates blood circulation and treats the symptoms of certain diseases. I had my lifestyle counsellor with me all the time, who guided me through the treatment. It was getting into a hot bath. The bath needed to be hot (104-110 degrees F) to accomplish this "fever" or "hydrotherapy" treatment.

The target was to obtain 102-105 degrees F oral body temperature and maintain it for 20-40 minutes, as tolerated. I started with 20 minutes and increased daily depending on how I coped.

When the oral body temperature goes above 100 degrees F or the patient begins to sweat, keep the head very cool with cold strips changed often. My lifestyle counsellor kept washcloths in ice cubes to keep them very cold.

She ensured that the bathwater was sufficient to maintain an oral temperature of 102-105 degrees F. Then, she drained the cooling water and added hot water as needed. The hot treatment ended with a tepid shower, brisk rubbing dry, and one hour of bed rest with a cold pack on the forehead.

4. Exercise Heals

We walked outside every morning through some woods and in the open. Sometimes it is a struggle to get up and go out for a walk. However, try it. It is incredible how you feel when you get back. I returned with so much energy, feeling revitalised, having spent some time outdoors! The walks were enjoyable for getting some exercise but also being out in the fresh air and sunshine.

5. Oxygen Heals

Cancer does not survive in an oxygenated environment. Oxygen has a powerful connection with cancer, so oxygen is a must-have. The oxygen molecules floating around in the air make up just 21% of our atmosphere. Hyperbaric oxygen therapy (HBOT) chambers tackle this by creating an enclosed, pressurised environment with air of up to 100% oxygen. The combination of high oxygen and atmospheric pressure takes oxygenation further by going beyond the red blood cells. They saturate the blood, plasma, and interstitial fluid with fresh oxygen, flooding every cellular corner and cranny with vital air. This boost in circulation enables nutrients and toxins to be transported as needed, and that helps swelling and inflammation, immunity, blood vessel growth, and stagnant tissues.

6. Sunshine Heals

Sunbathing in the garden was one of my favourite therapies. There was an enclosure made so I could lie and relax. A twenty to sixty-minute sunbath daily was helpful. I was exposing my face, arms, and operation site to the sun. This furnished the natural vitamin D and helped to lower cholesterol. Sunlight also increases the volume of oxygen in the blood.

As I sunbathed every afternoon, I contrasted that time with what I might have had to spend taking chemotherapy.

Fresh, outdoor air is so refreshing and is suitable for our health. Fresh air helps you heal faster, clear your lungs, improve your digestion, improve blood pressure and heart rate, strengthen the immune system, reduce obesity rates and strengthen family ties, all leading to a healthier you!

It may be challenging to avoid smog, motor exhaust, hydrocarbons, and tobacco smoke in the cities, so try to spend time out of cities as much as possible.

Being outdoors in fresh air is also an excellent time to take deep breaths down into your belly, as it is comfortable rather than the shallow breaths we usually take. If the weather is not very good, I still take twenty deep breaths outdoors or two to four times per day near an open window to encourage the oxygenation of tissues.

I always kept my bedroom well-ventilated but was careful not to sleep in a draft.

7. Gratitude Heals

Gratitude means thanks and appreciation. Expressing gratitude tends to spread positive feelings. You feel good about something, share that with others, and this makes someone else feel good. There are many benefits of practising gratitude. People who regularly practise gratitude by taking time to notice and reflect upon things they're thankful for will experience more positive emotions, feel more alive, sleep better, express more compassion and kindness, and even have more robust immune systems.

You can learn to be grateful for new things every day. This would mean that your attitude towards small and big things changes how you perceive situations by adjusting what you focus on.

I believe that gratitude is a special gift from God. It is about not taking things for granted. It is being thankful for what we have and receive. It allows us to cherish our present situation in ways that make us feel a sense of abundance rather than deprivation.

Lamentations 3:23-24, a book in the Bible, says: The steadfast love of the LORD never ceases; his mercies never come to an end; they are new every morning; great is your faithfulness. It is encouraging that God pours out His love for us and that His mercies are fresh daily. Every day is a new day in which we can move in a direction that defines our eternity.

Being vegan or eating plant-based is deemed to be healthier eating. However, you can be a 'junky vegan or vegetarian.' Many shop-bought plant-based alternatives are highly processed and packed with ingredients that may not even be recognisable.

I am delighted that so many people are moving towards plant-based eating, but there is another way to enjoy healthier plant-based foods. Staying close to nature and enjoying fresh produce rather than using heavily processed foods. Keep meals simple with lots of fruits, vegetables, nuts, and seeds. Choose from ingredients close to nature.

Having learnt the benefits of plant foods, it was essential to learn to love them to add to the diet daily. After returning from the 17-day recovery programme, I realised I had to make more interesting salads. I couldn't be eating lettuce, tomato, and cucumber every day! This was when I came across raw food. It opened up a whole new world. It was fun, exciting, and tasty. I was able to increase and enjoy more vegetables daily.

- dark leafy greens such as kale, spinach, Swiss chard, arugula
- broccoli sprouts
- cauliflower
- mushrooms
- purple cabbage
- red, yellow, and orange sweet pepper
- spring onions
- sunflower seeds, pumpkin seeds, almonds, or walnuts
- sprouted beans (mung beans, lentils)

This is one of the simple but substantial salads I made to include the different sources of cancer-fighting and prevention nutrients.

Start with the nutrient-rich dark leafy greens like kale and spinach, then add broccoli, the best source of liver detoxification, promoting sulforaphane and other anti-carcinogenic compounds.

Add the other vegetables like cauliflower, purple cabbage, red onion, leeks, red and yellow peppers, mushrooms, avocado, courgette (zucchini), sprouted seeds, nuts, and lentils. I would chop them up, sometimes finely and sometimes in chunks (to vary daily), and then mix them well with a great-tasting salad dressing.

Salad Dressing

I tried to keep the salad dressings simple and to include herbs and spices which were beneficial and readily available: Lemon juice, garlic, tahini, extra virgin olive oil or fresh olives, or cold-pressed flax oil.

Spices:

- oregano
- garlic powder
- turmeric powder
- cayenne pepper

Fresh herbs

- finely chopped coriander
- parsley
- basil
- chives
- spring onions

I made fresh vegetable juices to take in more greens, sometimes adding an apple, carrot, or beet to change the flavours.

As I think back over the years and my conversation with my oncologist, I am so happy that I stood my ground and looked at the various available options. I believe that decision protected me and helped me take responsibility for my health. Over the five years after my diagnosis, I had quarterly, six-monthly, and then yearly reviews with the consultants; however, none of the consultants wanted to know what I was doing differently, although they had concerns that I stayed away from mammograms and had not taken any of the other therapies that had been prescribed. As a result, my lifestyle improved, and I have not needed any medications or treatments other than implementing the simple health laws I learned. I shared them with my family, friends, and those motivated to make lifestyle changes and saw terrific positive results in their life too.

I enjoy sharing my experiences and letting people make choices about their health. We often know what we ought to do but don't know how to put it into practice. This is where our training is so necessary and will allow you to enjoy even more abundant and vibrant health.

We have created "The Amazing Wholistic Lifestyle Plan," which puts all these healing modalities into a simple system we learn and use daily. This helps optimise our health which protects us from lifestyle diseases and, where necessary, reverses lifestyle diseases.

Our bodies are beautifully and wonderfully made, and when given the proper nutrients and the right environment, they have the unique ability to heal themselves.

I discuss this in more detail in my book 'Amazing Health - 9 Principles of a Wholistic Lifestyle.' If you would like a copy of the book or would like me to speak at one of your events, please get in touch with me via email: at info@theamazinghealthbook.com or go to

www.theamazinghealthbook.com.

I sincerely hope you will take the simple steps to prioritise your overall health and wellness and enjoy life to the fullest. I have learnt to live a life of purpose. It did not happen overnight but by just taking one step at a time.

Don't let your health stop you from living your life to the fullest!

Enjoy Amazing Health.

About the Author

Naomi Watson, an international speaker, is passionate about health and well-being. She enjoys working with motivated people who want to change their lifestyles to overcome or protect themselves from lifestyle diseases.

Encountering cancer 15 years ago, Naomi chose to use natural adjunct therapies rather than chemotherapy and radiotherapy. On her quest to overcome health challenges and to gain a better life, Naomi now enjoys helping others transform themselves through whole food nutrition. Encouraging her clients to eat fresh fruits, vegetables, nuts, seeds, and herbs and through simple alternative healing modalities to feel tremendous and skyrocket their health!

Naomi recognises that although the health principles are simple, they can be challenging to put into practice without proper support. Having travelled to different countries to share her experiences, she observed people's eating habits and the availability of fruits and vegetables locally. She shares 'how' to increase fruits and vegetables in our diet, which helps improve the nutritional value of our meals.

Naomi was a wife to her late husband, mother to two beautiful sons and the primary carer for her late elderly parents. Here she learned to experiment and create healthy and tasty alternatives to their favourite foods using plant-based healthy ingredients; she appreciated her family's support in accepting her choice of nutrition. This has helped her to help children and adults to ease into healthy plant-based food in their daily lives to enjoy health.

Naomi trained and worked as a Management Accountant. Although she talked about health and lifestyle before her ordeal with cancer, she shares how individuals' responses changed after her recovery. She also noticed that although people agreed with what they should do, they were not doing it. That is when she started food demonstrations through which we could learn the simple and tasty ways of eating and enjoying a plant-based diet. She shares her vision of travelling and teaching this lifestyle to create fantastic health for those who want a more vibrant, abundant life.

Connect with Naomi:

naomi@theamazinghealthbook.com

www.TheAmazingHealthBook.com

LinkedIn.com/in/Naomi-Watson-04965819/

Forty Years of Nights Waking Up, Hard To Do

By Sharon Smith

My journey began several decades ago, aged 18 years of age. I had been accepted at the School of Nursing to undertake my Registered Nurse Training - Wow, lucky me, I thought. This involved a full medical, which included a routine check of my blood pressure. To my absolute horror and shock, but not totally surprised, I was informed I had high blood pressure. Horror because I was young and fit, shock because I was slim, and I thought healthy. Lack of surprise because my mother, her sister, seven brothers, and several cousins also suffered from this severe but common condition. Common to so many people of afro Caribbean descent.

Unfortunately, I just accepted the diagnosis and commenced the medication prescribed to lower it. I was informed it was a hereditary condition, usually known as essential hypertension, which was one of the major causes of early deaths or other debilitating conditions such as strokes and cardiovascular disease. I felt there was little I could personally do to make any radical changes to the outcome or progression of the disease. The condition could only be managed effectively by taking any appropriate medication prescribed. Additionally, I knew it was a long-term debilitating condition that would require strict compliance to control and prevent any serious damage to my heart, blood vessels, kidneys, and eyes. However, several tests were undertaken to exclude any underlying causes, and nothing was discovered, so the formal diagnosis was given, and the doctors were certain it was a genetic condition due to my family history.

Of course, I believed the doctors. My mother, grandparents, and other close members of her family had suffered from the same condition, including several who had died from arising complications. What was there to question? I told myself I was unlucky to have developed the condition at such an early age and fortunate to have been diagnosed early with access to effective treatment and excellent medical supervision, or so I thought. It strengthened my belief that I was entering the best professional body to acquire an excellent qualification with appropriate knowledge to help myself and my family. On reflection, I can see how deeply mistaken I was and deeply asleep, and so I did not hear or heed the first wake-up call of my body.

I studied and accepted the dictates I was taught, without any challenges, along with the 'healthy' foods of my parents, which I mistakenly thought was an exemplary diet. I was again mistaken. How could I possibly eat the same food my parents ate, prepared in a similar manner, and expect a different outcome? I believe that's called insanity! My parents had an allotment and grew a wide variety of greens, vegetables, and herbs. We juiced some of these greens and vegetables using a slow masticating juicer, which was unheard of then. I was always interested in health and helping others which was another reason why I did nursing, but sadly I was not fully aware of the truth, nor the depth of information kept from me. To enhance my health, I joined a gym and exercised regularly, doing yoga for relaxation and flexibility as well as more general cardiovascular activities. Nowhere in my training and practice was I told the benefits and importance of nutrition for health and that food could be used as medicine. I did have some basic information as my mother often made her own healthy remedies which she dispensed regularly and with quite some success.

My second 'wake-up call' came on the death of my beloved mother, aged 70 years young. She had followed all the medical advice given, taking a plethora of pharmaceutical drugs to keep that stubborn high blood pressure of hers (Idiopathic hypertension) under control, as it was not curable. She was so pleased she had lived to the ripe old age of 65 as all her eight siblings died well before her. Reaching the age of 60 from this debilitating and 'silent killer' was a victory to celebrate. She always gave thanks and was surprised to still be alive. She planned her 60th birthday party tentatively as she didn't want to "tempt fate" (her own words), as she really did not believe she would make it. We celebrated her sixtieth birthday with joy, style, and thanksgiving, an occasion many take for granted. The silent killer had stayed silent. Several years later, she was diagnosed with polycystic kidney, then kidney failure, from which she went on to have regular dialysis. This we accepted stoically, and she lived her life as best as she could despite the severe restrictions this placed on her daily life and undertakings. Tragically, she had a massive cerebral haemorrhage, aged 70 years young, from which she never woke.

On reflection, I realised that was another 'Wake-Up call.' I felt perturbed, something was not quite right, but I could not say exactly what it was. It was just a deep feeling of disquiet and unhappiness in addition to loss and grief. It had me questioning why, as I asked both myself and the doctors so many questions as to how and why it had happened, not least being, do I want to go down this same path where why my mother had died despite strictly following medical guidance and advice, and taking the plethora of prescribed drugs? She often joked that she would rattle if she was held up and shaken because she was taking so many. Never once was there any mention that the many medications she had been prescribed could have any unwanted or adverse effects. The perpetual escalation of her medication and condition was accepted as inevitable, and neither she; the family; nor myself did anything to investigate or challenge this medical rhetoric. Our culture conditioned us to accept our doctor's word as gospel, but I felt something was not right.

Not knowing where else to turn for answers, I prayed many prayers and cried an ocean of tears when I understood my prayers were finally being answered. I was invited to a health workshop on making a variety of nut milks at home and the many health benefits and cost-effectiveness it gave. So began my long slow journey and ultimate awakening. I was able to ask myself, whose beliefs are these anyway? Were they true? Were most of the sicknesses and diseases mainly due to the genes we inherited from our families, or due to the fact, often unconsciously, that we are living and following similar lifestyles, eating the same diet, following similar practices, and accepting similar self-limiting beliefs? Nurture versus nature? What evidence was there to support these arguments? So why do we believe, trust, and accept what we are told?

Wake up, I said to myself, wake up! No more, I decided that this was not my reality. Now I can see how this conditioning is stopping many from seeking and finding alternative solutions. This programming is disempowering and has been happening for far too long, and so we believe our family's history, our culture, the media, and continuing misinformation keeps us from coming together and sharing our stories of healing, the traditional use of medicinal herbs, and our own experience of what works for us. When you are young, you believe what you are told unquestioningly. Thus began my life's journey, filled with passion and purpose in a search for deeper understanding and alternative options for natural remedies for those and myself who did not wish to use only prescribed pharmaceuticals. I finally accepted that I wanted to make a difference and that continuing on the old and easy path with lethargy and fear and taking the many medications could lead to certain death. So even feeling lost, disempowered, and too afraid to take back control of my own health and make radical changes would also be like failing my mother all over again. No, I said to myself, you must change your mindset and your way of life, and yes, take back control, so you don't die early and can live a life of joy and vitality, as is our birthright. I'm now a passionate advocate for those needing support in speaking with their GP to try a number of lifestyle changes, such as the reduction of medication and commencing exercising.

I really hope that by sharing this information with you, along with my life's journey and many wake-up calls, will not only be your wake-up call but will empower you to seek and strive to cast aside some of these limiting beliefs and disempowering programming and find the answers to your needs for your own healing.

My personal and final wake-up call from my body was when I woke up one summer day in a daze on a park bench surrounded by paramedics and members of the public. I was startled, and I wondered what was happening. My vital signs were being checked by a medic, and someone was asking me my name and if I was ok. I answered slowly, saying my name as I attempted to sit up, but I was gently restrained. I was told to lie still and gently pushed back down, which I did reluctantly, full of embarrassment. Can you imagine, I was embarrassed! I was embarrassed to have passed out cold and been a bother to others. As I regained consciousness, my memories slowly came back to me. I was taken to A & E and admitted with hypotension. I did not dare admit I had stopped taking my medication and had only taken it prior to visiting my GP. Wow, I had to ask myself, did I really want to continue down this path of denial and compliance? Yes, I was at a critical crossroads; a choice had to be made.

Ask yourself, where do your programming and beliefs come from? What can you do to empower and overcome this placid acceptance and, in many instances, paralyzing fears which keep us from searching and believing that if the experts and science do not know the answers, then who are we to find them? We are not a product of our past, shaped by culture and our ancestors. This is not the whole story and is so disempowering, and it's been happening for far too long. Just because something is passed down through our families for many generations does not make it inevitable, so I hope my story will have you questioning these beliefs. Whose beliefs are they, anyway? My beliefs are that YOU, and not your genes, are in control of your health. Genetics or epigenetics?

In support of this journey, I can honestly say I woke up this morning feeling vibrant and healthy. I said to myself, yes, I have taken back control and have full responsibility for my health and my life, not leave it to the medical and pharmaceutical industry, whose first port of call is drugs and suppression of symptoms. In awakening, literally and figuratively, I realized that there is a natural law of health not taught in the Schools of Nursing. Many, like myself, have been led astray by deviating from the natural laws of health and hygiene. I now believe that radical resilience, not disease, is our body's destiny.

So began the journey for answers to my disease and how to self-care to heal. I sought answers, read many books, attended many natural health seminars, and came to understand that within every cell of the body is the ability to heal, regenerate, or self-destruct where necessary in the interest of the body as a whole. We are not compartmentalized, as medicine has segregated the different body parts into a specialism. We are holistic beings, and the body works cohesively as a whole. Every part is connected, and if one part malfunctions, then there is either a problem upstream or downstream. Nothing happens in isolation, within the body, and our bodies are attempting to alert us by these signs and symptoms. My goal is to listen to my body and hear what it is trying to tell me, in addition to listening to the teachers and asking questions for deeper understanding. I use all my senses to ensure the information resonates with my innate understanding and wisdom. No longer will I sit passively and absorb information like a sponge. Where necessary, I am going to ask questions and challenge where necessary for clarification. The aim was to learn, discover, and collaborate with others of a similar mindset. From that moment, I made this decision to learn to heal myself and activate my body's natural healing ability; I challenged myself to put into practice what I learned. As I wish to improve my own health and that of others, I promised myself that every year I would keep refining and learning new things about improving my health by using food as medicine. My passion lies in helping others along this self-healing journey by offering my knowledge, assistance, and support, where necessary, to prevent pain, unnecessary suffering, and untimely deaths. As I travel down this path of natural health and well-being, I no longer worry about the rhetoric of mainstream doctors and their limiting beliefs and practices. Knowledge is power if applied.

On my healing journey, I discovered a multitude of important and different modalities, basic principles, and many practices that can heal the body and assist us in health instead of masking and suppressing symptoms or poisoning the body when used.

Here are just a few of the basic principles and a few tools I used on my journey, though by no means all, to gain natural healing and enhanced health.

The breath of life, breathing deeply, and using the diaphragm is critical as life cannot be maintained for any length of time if we have no breath left in us. Breathe outside in the fresh air and turn to nature for balance and health. Adequate sunshine is a part of this.

Hydration is critical for health, and there is much evidence supporting the importance of drinking adequate amounts of clean, pure water. We are 60 – 75 percent water and must drink to replace all water used or lost through normal bodily function. Remove or reduce all additives to the water you drink by filtering it, lest you become the filter. This includes the water you bathe in.

The importance of sleep is critical for rest and repair of the body. Aim to have 7 – 8 hrs sleep each night for overall health and enhanced brain function. In addition, eating a whole food plant diet is optimum for your health.

Exercising on a regular basis is good for the body. It enhances insulin sensitivity and lowers the incidence of metabolic disease and diabetes and should not be taken for granted.

Eat an abundance of plant food, nutrient-dense and calorie poor. Avoid packaged food which appears convenient in the short term but is highly detrimental to health, with many hidden dangers such as sugar and seed oils. Both are poisonous to the body. Eat a moderate amount of cold-pressed organic oils, such as virgin olive oil, coconut oil, hemp seed oil, and nut oils.

My mantra is, 'let food be thy medicine, and there will be no need for medicine.' Always remember, you are what you eat and what you eat eats! All meat should be consumed in moderation, pasture-raised and organic if eaten at all. Eating real food is superior to supplements. Ideally, food should be Fresh; Raw; Organic; Green; and Seasonal wherever possible. So, remember to eat your FROGS, and do your best so you can spring for your highest health. You deserve it.

Faith, prayer, family, and friends are also important parts of the equation.

I am thrilled by the many benefits this healthier lifestyle and in-depth knowledge have afforded me. There are so many benefits, I am unable to count them, and no real side effects. It does take effort, time, and commitment, but I can truly say it is worth the effort.

I rise in the morning with anticipation, joy, exuberance, and enough energy to power my way through the day with zest. My hereditary blood pressure of 230/140 on my crisis admission to the hospital at the start of my journey is now 140/80 - 135/85 without medication. I do not need to diet, and my weight remains steady. I eat intuitively, without restriction, with thorough enjoyment, and the full knowledge of what is good for me and my health. I listen to my body when it speaks. I am not obsessive and follow an 80/20 principle. I ensure I eat a wide and varied diet, high in dietary fiber, to promote excellent gut health and the prevention of constipation. Being better informed, with heightened awareness, of the importance of our gut health in relation to maintaining our immunity and overall health, I give it my full attention.

Eating out with family and friends is important for me, so I do eat out on special occasions to celebrate life without any feelings of guilt. Family and friends are a blessing in our life and should be celebrated. They do not all follow my lifestyle, but they see the benefits, and I let them know about my eating lifestyle without pushing it down their throat. It is so important to enjoy your food and eat without guilt. Bless it, enjoy It, and only good will come from all that you put into your body. Just start the journey with faith and intention and believe you can, particularly with support and guidance.

Thank you so much for taking the time to read about my journey. I appreciate it. Now, will you join me on my continuing journey and wake up? The time for sleep is long past, and you deserve to be the best you can be. We are children of God and the universe, and we are promised good health in all things if we follow his principles and obey the laws of health. I wish you success, vibrant health, and happiness.

About the Author

Sharon is both a UK State Registered Nurse and a Paediatric children's nurse. She spent over 30yrs as a neonatal nurse with Guys & St Thomas Hospital, one of the UK's leading providers of hospital and community-based healthcare, research and education. Where she specialised in caring for very sick and premature babies. She is therefore fully qualified and conversant with the medical model of health.

She has also dedicated the last 15 years to studying naturopathic health and nutrition. Completing many courses on the subject, the last undertaken with the Church as a medical missionary. The course covered the natural laws of health and its implementation in today's society. She is therefore fully conversant with both models of health, allopathic and naturopathic.

Her passion is particularly for women's, health recognising that with raised awareness and guidance they can make the choice to add so many more years to their life as well as life to their years. The common diseases that are so prevalent in our society today can be prevented as well as reversed and using nutrition and natural remedies.

Sharon recognizes that everyone, can and must take control of their own health, if both they and their family are to prevent the scourge of dis-ease that is overwhelming everyday life today: metabolic syndrome, diabetes, high blood pressure, obesity, prostate and breast cancer, and poor gut health that is so prevalent, all for lack of knowledge and miss-information which distracts us from the basic principles and foundation of health.

She feels it is such a tragedy that so many people are sleep walking into poor health, lethargy and an early grave. Knowing that these diseases and symptoms of poor health are all easily preventable and reversible, breaks her heart.

The main aim of her work is to educate and empower individuals to take back control of their health. To support this she has developed several flagship products conducive to the gut biome and therefore to overall health and wellness using live cultures. They are easy to produce at home, taste great in addition to been healthy, nutritious, and easy to digest.

Her clients are continually inspired as they discover new ways to increase energy, detoxify the body, boost immunity, reduce food allergies and other digestive problems as they begin eating more; natural, plant-based wholefoods, full of Pre and probiotics, organic and delicious.

Sharon says give the body what it needs and it will heal itself. She asks nothing of you she does not or will not do herself.

Sharon's motto is: "To achieve better health for all - I walk the the talk so my clients can live the dream."

Connect with Sharon:

Shas@mysistershealth.com

www.MySistersHealth.com

www.LinkedIn.com/in/Sharon-Smith-287449b3/

The authors are proud to support the African Women's Empowerment Forum (AWEF), helping them in their mission to support their members, who come from a variety of African countries and the Diaspora, including Zimbabwe, Ghana, Nigeria and Jamaica.

In the United Kingdom, African women, who are or were refugees and asylum seekers have few opportunities to become self-sufficient, hence there is a dependency on charity or welfare for their basic survival. The loss of being self-supporting denies them the opportunity of having self-confidence, it also deprives them of their pride of accomplishment. Living in these demotivated conditions more often than not leads to negative effects psychologically, socially and even mentally.

The African Women Empowerment Forum CIC [AWEF] was founded by Faith Gakanje-Ajala to develop and deliver an accessible empowerment process to give African Women, Refugees, Asylum Seekers and their children the power of making decisions on their own, through having access to information and resources that will enhance and facilitate their ability to make the self-directed, life enhancing decisions that unlock the options and opportunities from which they can make choices for themselves.

AWEF, supported by it's Patrons, Members, Partners and Sponsors, provides opportunities for our Women to learn skills for self-improvement and personal, social and entrepreneurial development, changing their own and others' perceptions through democratic means.

Then with these abilities they become more and more able to exercise assertiveness within collective decision-making processes allowing them to generate ongoing, practical and effective growth in their lives.

AWEF runs workshops and seminars throughout the year for our members and community. For example, our exciting Green Week Agenda Campaign, which includes the Green & Black Event to raise awareness on how climate change impacts the BAME community, marking the celebration of Black History Month and the contribution of the BAME community to Nottingham and the East Midlands.

For more information and to find out how you can assist The African Women Empowerment Forum CIC, please reach out to:

Web: info@awef.org.uk
Phone: 07425 580561

Printed in Great Britain
by Amazon